THE CLIMATE FOR LEARNING

THE CLIMATE
FOR LEARNING

Mike Torbe & Peter Medway

BOYNTON/COOK PUBLISHERS, INC.

This book was first published in 1981 as the core book of the Language, Teaching and Learning series (General Editor: Mike Torbe). It is reprinted by arrangement with the original publishers, Ward Lock Educational, London, England.

Acknowledgment

The publishers and authors are grateful to Thomas Nelson & Sons Ltd. (publishers) for permission to reprint the extract from M. B. V. Roberts's *Biology: A Functional Approach* (1976)

For information address Boynton/Cook Publishers, Inc.
206 Claremont Avenue, Montclair, NJ 07042

ISBN: 0-86709-041-3   (original ISBN: 0-7062-4103-7)

Printed in the United States of America

82 83 84 85 86   10 9 8 7 6 5 4 3 2 1

Contents

Authors' Note

In this book, you will see examples of teachers and students talking, writing, reading, teaching and learning. The people whose words and experiences we quote come from Bristol, Coventry, Enfield, several parts of London, Nottingham, Sheffield, Wakefield and Warwickshire. Many of them are part of our personal teaching histories: we thank them for leaving their words with us.

Although everything in the book, apart from the words of others, originated in the words of one or other of us, most of it can't now be unscrambled into the work of either. But where one of us reported a personal experience or response, we saw no point in forcing it into the semblance of a joint statement. So among the 'we's', the reader will sometimes encounter an 'I'.

Readers outside the United Kingdom may like to know that secondary schooling in the UK usually starts at the age of eleven, is compulsory for five years (until the statutory school-leaving age of sixteen) and continues in the 'sixth' form for one or two years for those who wish to stay on to take further exams.

THE CLIMATE
FOR LEARNING

Preface

This book, and the series of which it is a part, *Language, Teaching and Learning*, is meant to show why some teachers find it worth while to put their ideas about language and learning into practice. The books suggest how the ideas apply to actual teaching and learning, and show what the resulting children's language looks like. They try, that is, to document, rather than philosophize.

There are two things about 'language across the curriculum' which make it different from traditional good practice. One is the idea of teachers collaborating with each other, whatever their subjects or main interests, because of a shared belief that the way pupils use their language to learn is much the same, whatever the learning is about. Even though there are clearly some kinds of learning which have little to do with language – for instance some aspects of mathematical thinking, some learning of physical skills, some leaps of intuition in all areas that seem to bypass language – it is equally clear that there is a great deal which could not happen without language. First acquaintance with most ideas, for example, is made through reading or being told about something; and as the series as a whole will argue, it is by talking, writing, reading and listening that learners come to understand ideas. Thus it is not enough to look at the formal aspects of language in education – the books people read, and the lectures they listen to: we must also take care to acknowledge the students' own talk as a way by which they come to understand, and consider the writing and reading they will necessarily do if they are to be successful.

The other main notion of 'language across the curriculum' is the way in which pupils are invited to share in understanding the processes of learning, and thus learn to accept responsibility for the manner and quality of their own learning. When teachers demystify the means of learning, and make explicit to learners what the processes are, then both parties in education are actively participating: the student needs to be as personally engaged as the teacher is, if the learning is to be successful.

The influence of the Bullock Report (DES 1975) has been considerable; but what it actually said about the 'policy for language across the curriculum' that every school should have, was fairly vague:

> We must convince the teacher of history or of science, for example, that he has to understand the process by which his pupils take possession of the historical or scientific knowledge that is offered them; and that such an understanding involves his paying attention to the part language plays in learning.

It was not made clear, though, how that convincing should be achieved. The implied assumption was that all that was necessary was to display the evidence, and 'teachers of history or of science' would instantly be persuaded by the obvious truths of the ideas. Clearly, it was always going to be more complicated than that. Most secondary teachers feel that their first allegiance is to their subject, and that 'language' is the province of the English teacher. For them to begin to 'pay attention to the part language plays in learning' there is a degree of convincing needed, but not in the way implied by the Bullock Report, where 'convincing' suggested the presentation of facts by an informed party to uninformed listeners or readers. No: teachers need to *feel* convinced in their own minds that it's worth bothering with these ideas at all; that if they do try to 'pay attention' to language, the effort will be worth it because pupils will learn more.

The series therefore looks at 'language and learning' in two main ways. This core book considers basic theories, and puts them into the context of school learning in general, irrespective of the subject. The other books begin from the perspective of the teacher of particular subjects: the assumption is that in most readers' minds there will be the question 'When I teach my subject what have these ideas about language and learning to do with me?' A subject teacher may not have an overview of the life of a school; but a child may, in the course of one day at school, meet six or more different teachers teaching as many different subjects, each making different language demands on the learner. The kind of writing demanded in RE or science may be totally different from the writing required in history or English. A 'discussion' in geography can be very different from a 'discussion' in maths. These varying experiences together create that aspect of school we can call its 'language life', but the total language life of a child at school is not visible to any one teacher. There is little opportunity for teachers to become familiar with what happens to pupils in other subjects, unless they take part in team teaching. The pupil passes through the whole experience, but the teacher is only familiar with a small part of it. The books therefore are also intended to introduce the general reader to some of the implications of looking at teaching and learning from the point of view of subjects, and to give some flavour of what happens in classrooms in our schools.

I do not make any grand claims for these books. They represent a first hesitant attempt to look systematically at the idea of 'language across the curriculum' and to see what can happen to individual teachers if they take the idea seriously.

Mike Torbe
General Editor

Note

For the reference of readers not familiar with the English educational system a list follows of the corresponding school years and ages of children in secondary school:

First year: 11–12 years old
Second year: 12–13 years old
Third year: 13–14 years old
Fourth year: 14–15 years old
Fifth year: 15–16 years old
Lower sixth: 16–17 years old
Upper sixth: 17–18 years old

The Background

In 1969, I read, on someone's recommendation, a book called *The Anatomy of Judgement* by M. J. L. Abercrombie. It excited me enormously. It dealt with the effects of perception upon learning, and with the way in which people will defend their perceptions as though they are crucially important to them. Dr Abercrombie had developed a fascinating technique: she posed her students a problem and requested them to commit themselves to a point of view on it, by writing down a definition or explanation or whatever; then, with that commitment on paper before them, they discussed the basic problem. Her book included transcripts of some of the discussions, and considered what individuals did in talk, how, why, and under what circumstances people changed their point of view, and what the role of the teacher-chairman was. Her students were medical students, not school pupils, but the effect upon my own teaching was, and has remained, far-reaching.

At more or less the same time I read *Language, the Learner and the School* (Barnes *et al.* 1971). If Abercrombie's book had excited me, this one, especially Douglas Barnes's analysis of teacher-talk, crucified me. Everything I had ever done and felt uneasy about was anatomized for me; as Penny Blackie (1971) put it 'I saw with guilty recognition how it all applied to me'. Its demonstration of the way a teacher can *prevent* learning rather than generate it, by the way he or she talks to the pupils and allows them to respond, was devastating: its innocent opening statement became a depthcharge which didn't just explode once, but went on exploding: 'This paper is concerned with part of the teacher's behaviour, his language, and some of its effects upon his pupils.' So too did the explanation of how the study had been effected. His students, Barnes reported, had, 'tape-recorded first-year lessons taught by friends, transcribed them, and analysed them according to a scheme I supplied. The teachers participating found this an enlightening and disturbing task.'

The book provided a kind of toolkit for my own teaching for the next ten years – and not just for me, I think. It also, in that mysterious way a book read at the right time will do, acted as a catalyst to synthesize a whole range of other ideas I had collected, partly from other reading and partly from considering my own experience.

Between all those ideas, with Barnes and Abercrombie as my main mentors, I was able to turn my classrooms into laboratories in which, together, we could explore, experiment with, and theorize about learning and its relationship with talk; because it seemed clear that what happens in talk is crucial to the learning of the talker. For the first time everything was making me look seriously at what I'd previously taken for granted, and indeed generally seen as a necessary nuisance, and something I'd have to put up with: the talk that my pupils did *whether I wanted them to or not*. Once I saw its importance and its inevitability, I stopped trying to prevent it, and tried instead to create contexts in which talk became the way in which pupils did what had to be done. The powerful thrust to share ideas and to test out new thinking, and to do it in the most natural and comfortable way – through talk – was something to be used and built on, not fought against. The taping of lessons and the transcribing of the tapes – enormously laborious, but as rewarding as it was arduous – gave a clear picture of the learning events of the classroom. Transcribing necessitates playing stretches of tape over and over, to grasp one segment accurately, and as you do this, more and more is revealed: the way the teacher talks too much, and so often talks over the pupils; the way one pupil dominates others; the way one pupil returns time and time again, unheeded, to a preoccupation; the way what one person says, clear and obvious enough, is nevertheless completely misunderstood by everyone else; and so on. The more I listened to the tapes, the less I talked in class, and the more my teaching energies went into devising contexts in which the learners' talk could take place naturally and fluidly, without my having to interfere with it.

What I learned about talk, I had to relearn about writing, and then, much later, about reading. Writing bothered me, as a language process, because I couldn't see how it could tap the individual's learning as directly as talk. But the Writing Research Unit at the London Institute, the group that was running the Schools Council Project *The Development of Writing Abilities*, showed me a way through. Its 'language function model' demonstrated a way of looking at writing which not only straddled all the subjects of the curriculum, but also, with its (to me) brand new notion of 'expressive language', indicated a kind of writing I wanted to encourage, with its 'relationship to thinking (p. 11) . . . the means by which the new is tentatively explored. . . . exploratory situations seem to call for it. . . . [it is] a kind of matrix from which differentiated forms of mature writing are developed (p. 83). . . . the kind of writing that might be called "thinking aloud on paper" (p. 89). . . . the kind best adapted to exploration and discovery (p. 197)' (all references to Britton 1975).

In the event, the other axis of the research has been perhaps more influential: the categorization of audience, and its demonstration of what I suppose most good teachers knew intuitively, but hadn't seen so clearly expressed: that the audience categories 'represent a relationship between writer and reader' and that

> in school . . . it is almost always the teacher who defines the writing and who does so by defining a writing task with more or less explicitness. Not only does he define the task, but also nominates himself as audience. He is not, however, simply a one-man audience but also the sole arbiter, appraiser, grader and judge of the performance. . . . The writer is frequently placed in the position of telling the reader what the latter already knows more fully and more deeply. (Britton 1975, p. 64)

The outcome of this particular thread of experience, interweaving with the other threads, again threw my teaching into disorder. I could and did devise ways of encouraging my pupils to write expressively – logbooks about their reading and thinking, running commentaries, letters to me or to each other and so on. But then how was I to deal with the writing? I could hardly tick and grade a letter to me in which a pupil had addressed me directly, personally and in confidence. A letter to me demanded a letter in reply: a logbook, with thoughts caught on the point of the pen, demanded the courtesy of responses to those thoughts, not to the handwriting or spelling. The more pupils trust the teacher enough to want to write openly, the more important it becomes to find ways of responding that will

7

continue and extend the kinds of relationships that are developing. So pupils' writing becomes part of a dialogue; but whereas teacher–pupil dialogue in class is generally public and shared, the dialogue about, and in, writing often remains private between the one pupil and the teacher, and sometimes is never even mentioned in talk at all. For some pupils, the personal relationship in writing is more rewarding than a relationship face-to-face.

Some of my colleagues were also engaged, either individually or together, in similar explorations. A science teacher, another English teacher, a sociology teacher, a maths teacher – all of them had in common a concern for their pupils' learning. They didn't begin by being concerned with language, but found that listening to the pupils' talk, looking at their writing, and considering their reading, as well as thinking increasingly carefully about what they themselves were saying – these offered insights into the ways students were learning.

And then in 1975 came the Bullock Report, *A Language for Life* (DES 1975), and what had been a personal concern for a few colleagues became suddenly a topic of national interest:

> We strongly recommend that whatever the means chosen to implement it a policy for language across the curriculum should be adopted by every secondary school. (12.12, p. 193)

Schools and local authorities, stirred by Chapter 12 of the Bullock Report more than any other, looked for help in doing exactly what was asked of them – implementing a policy. But what is a language policy? And how shall it be implemented?

The notion of 'a policy' implies that what the individual teacher has perceived about his or her own teaching can be integrated with what other teachers are doing. A policy for 'language across the curriculum' then is

> a series of strategies in the classroom and in the whole school, and a *process* – of discussion, of asking questions, and finding answers to those questions. Once begun, the process continues permanently. . . . [It] is an attempt to develop a shared set of intentions about how teachers might best assist their pupils to learn. (Torbe 1976)

Some of what individual teachers had perceived has already been described, but the concentration on talk had had several effects. Perhaps the main one was to loosen several of the invisible bonds that had previously chained teachers. If what Vygotsky and Piaget, George Kelly and Sapir, D. W. Harding and Cassirer (and all the others) said was true, that we learn by talking, and that learning is an act of creation by which we make and shape the very world we inhabit, then that meant the *pupils* had to do the talking, not the teachers. Thus, teachers had to become listeners, paying attention to what their pupils were trying to do in talk, accepting their present understandings and building on them so that learners could make the information they were presented with into comprehended knowledge. It meant, therefore, establishing fundamentally different relationships between teacher and learner: you can only maintain authoritarian relationships by controlling the talk, by permitting particular kinds of discourse and address, and outlawing others; but these new ideas meant the *learner* had to choose the kinds of talk which are necessary. As soon as teachers began to put pupils in teacherless groups and to listen attentively to the pupils talking, or to tapes of what pupils said in such groups, then a radical shift in the teacher–pupil relationship inevitably occurred.

It wasn't only in talk that there was this shift of perspective. The Writing Research Unit at the London Institute paid the same kinds of attention to writing that was already being paid to talk. The results were as striking and as influential as the previous work had been. Not only did their 'function model' direct attention in new ways to the differing varieties of writing available, but the emphasis given to the three major functions of writing – communication, shaping, and *learning* – brought home the idea that the product of writing may involve an act of communication, but the process of writing is, or should be, an act of learning. When the researchers added to that the dimension of audience, and showed so clearly how writing varies in content, form and in quality depending on who it's written for (Rosen 1973, McLeod 1976) then there was the sense of a circle being completed: in writing, too, there were ways in which relationships had to change. If a teacher encourages pupils to write letters to authors, to keep diaries and logbooks, to write poems and stories about science experiments, to keep a book for private writing, or to think aloud on paper as a running commentary, then such writing cannot be marked and graded like a formal essay. So how shall it be received and responded to? The answer to that question took teachers into yet newer kinds of relationships, as *Writing and Learning across the Curriculum 11–16* (Martin *et al.* 1976) demonstrated.

The theory behind 'language across the curriculum' concerns what happens to learners faced with many of the kinds of learning common to education, and the ways their language helps them to engage with and comprehend the matter being tackled. But there is a paradox inherent in the way the idea has been discussed, because inevitably the 'learner' in question has been seen as the school or college student. There has been an assumption that if the student is the learner, then the teacher must be someone who is not a learner. Clearly, though, the ideas of 'language across the curriculum', complex and difficult as they may be, imply that the teacher too must become learner in order to make sense of the theory and transmute it into practice. The teacher already knows about the 'subject' he or she is teaching, but now has to learn how that knowledge is best learnt by the pupils. What kinds of classroom experience will most encourage learning? What can I do to help my pupils? And how can I find out if it's worked or not? This kind of learning isn't a matter of information being presented and accepted. Really, the 'information' doesn't even exist, in one sense. There are only the raw data of classroom events, the pages of writing, the hours and minutes of talk, the books and worksheets that are read. The data can only become information – 'knowledge' – when they are worked on and interpreted by the teacher.

In this book, we try and present the language events of the classroom, offer a way of inspecting and making sense of them, and propose a basic approach to teaching and learning in the light of the theories that underlie language across the curriculum. There is one major, and deliberate, omission. We have left uninvestigated the question of that learning that undoubtedly occurs alongside 'educational' learning: the learning about one's social identity, and one's place in the scheme of things. It is the complex area of what happens to children labelled in any way – 'remedial' or 'naughty' or 'bright': the hidden rather than the visible curriculum of our education system. It is the way messages about one's ability and potential are conveyed subtly or obviously through the language of an institution, the kinds of topic discussed often, by Jackson and Marsden (1966),

David Hargreaves (1967, 1975), Michael F. D. Young (1974) and many others. It is omitted not because we are unaware of it but because our concern is the positive one of showing that most pupils can, contrary to what is commonly supposed, make something useful for themselves out of the knowledge and ideas which are the *declared* business of education. We hope that one outcome of reading this book might be that readers feel 'Perhaps my pupils too can learn like this'. Some of the students whose work you will see could have been disabled by being adversely labelled. Instead, their teachers refused to stereotype, and made them successful by creating a certain kind of climate in their classrooms. Some of the elements in this climate were particular uses of talking, writing, listening and reading, and it is these which we seek to identify in this book.

Generalizations

I

On a hot sunny afternoon in June, a second-year class in a comprehensive school in the Midlands is doing science. They are working in small groups, each with a tape-recorder, answering questions from a worksheet about food-chains. Barney and Alan have struggled with the questions. They have tried asking the teacher, but she wants them to make the final judgments themselves, so, though she's helped, she's not given them the answers.

Teacher	If all the lettuce had gone, what would the rabbit live on?
Alan	Wheat
Teacher	Wheat
Alan	And water
Teacher	Anything else?
Barney	Greenfly – no
Alan	No, ladybirds
Barney	Or sparrows

The whole thing confuses them, and they are unable to find their way through what is to them the impenetrable maze of the diagram they are working from. Mary sits at the same table, but they don't let her join in with them: they say she's a girl, and fat, and a bit deaf. But they know she can answer these questions – she's good at work. She tried to ask something herself, but the teacher is intent on Barney and Alan.

Mary	Miss, what –
Teacher	Which arrows are pointing to the rabbit?
Barney	Er, wheat and lettuce and cats
Teacher	Is that pointing to rabbits?
Alan ⎫ *Barney* ⎭	Yeah

Alan	It's going straight down
Barney	It's going there
Mary	(*in amazement*) Rabbits eat cats?
Barney	(*fiercely*) Don't laugh
Alan	Cats eat mouse. Look, mouse, cats
Barney	Shut up, we're not talking about that

The teacher leaves them, and Barney, giving up the attempt to answer the questions himself, decides to interview Mary. There are some moments of friction ('Come on, Carrots, come on,' he says, and 'Shut up you,' snaps Mary) but gradually, instead of the despairing but brash incompetence he showed earlier, there's a change and he becomes involved, to the extent of poring over the diagram with Mary. Helped by her, he sorts out the implications of food-chains.

Barney	(*reading from sheet*) Could you say something about the number of greenfly compared to the number of cats – the number of cats compared to the number of owls?
Mary	Hmmm, well, there are more greenflies than cats actually – hang on a minute, let's have a look. Yeah, because a cat, right, the cat has only got one thing to feed on, hasn't it?
Barney	What's that? Sparrows?
Mary	Look, mouse
Barney	And sparrows
Mary	Well, you know, but –
Barney	The cat can feed on the sparrows and . . . on the mouse . . .
Mary	Yeah, but there are more greenflies because it's got lettuce, wheat and grass, and really there are more greenflies than cats
Barney	Well if . . . the cats die the sparrows will increase more, 'cos the cat eat more sparrows than mouse, 'cos the cats can't find mouse 'cos they hide. . . .

This kind of discussion is different enough from the faintly hopeless answers the teacher was getting; but at the end of the taped conversation, something else happens. Barney reads the last question, and Mary's answer takes them both clear away from their hot classroom, along a logical chain to an important generalization:

Barney   Can you think of any reason why people try to save endangered animals from being ex – extinct?

Mary   Because if one of those animals dies, obviously the other animals will have less food to feed on, right? And that food-chain is getting more dangerous, and less and less, and we're one of those food-chains, we're in part of that food-chain, so we hope they'll be all right

Why do we say this is an 'important' generalization? Well, once you have grasped the idea that anything that affects an individual link in a food-chain affects the whole chain, you don't have to work out the idea separately for each food-chain you come across. So a generalization is a statement of a pattern. It is a powerful thing to acquire because although you may have generated it by thinking about one particular case, it will enable you to think about all such cases in general.

Making a generalization can be a kind of summing-up; it can come as a sudden insight. Mary hasn't exactly managed to articulate the one that she and Barney are on the edge of; but it might be expressed: 'Food-chains are about dependency: human beings are part of a food-chain, and anything that affects part of the chain affects us too.' Once patterns like that are perceived, even dimly, then learning stops being a chore. On the tape, the quality of the voices changes: the serious tone of voice of both speakers, the tentativeness, and the note of recognition, indicate that the pupils have now become active seekers after the understanding of these difficult new ideas. The power of the generalization, with its patterning of experience and its sense of a satisfying insight, is what animates their learning. Establishing a generalization counts as a successful conclusion to a search.

II

The transcript of the food-chain lesson displays other features that are of significance, as well as the way it culminates in a generalization. In a way, it lays out the agenda for a good deal of what this book is to be about.

Firstly, the learners themselves are at the centre of the experience, and not the teacher. Rightly; since the purpose of 'education' lies in what happens to the pupils, although she has worked hard to create the context for their learning.

Secondly, the learners know other things as well as what

they've learnt in these lessons (or indeed, in school at all), and they have to draw on that knowledge in order to understand the new knowledge implicit in the theoretical model that is a food-chain. The food-chain abstracts one strand from the complexity of real-life experience – the notion of dependency – but unless Barney and Mary have some previous knowledge, it won't make sense. For instance, they need to know that cats do eat mice.

Thirdly, they reach their complex generalization by talking not like Nobel prize-winners, or biology textbooks, but the way children do talk. In other words, their 'learning' grows out of their own language, and their language resources are perfectly adequate for them to make the perception that they do. They don't *need* to talk like the textbook: they can learn perfectly successfully with what they've got. Teachers can work within that boundary, and yet attain major conceptual advances in pupils; and as that happens, so the boundaries of the pupils' language will become extended.

The fourth point is that what happens is a product of a particular style of teaching, in which the teacher sets up a situation in a way that shows insight into the learning process. What we observe the children doing is puzzling out the significance of the knowledge that is being presented to them, and being given the time and space to do it. The puzzling out is necessary because the knowledge is presented in a sort of code – in a diagram, in fact. Such a representation of knowledge can't be converted instantly to knowledge in a child's head. It has to be worked on to give up its meaning, because at the moment it's a diagram of a theoretical abstraction – a model.

Why not shortcircuit the process by telling them? Here, we reach towards the heart of the argument. This teacher has avoided the assumption that if she did tell them, if she 'explained' the knowledge, that would be different and more accessible than presenting it in code, in a diagram. The knowledge would still be in code, because it would be in language. 'Human beings are part of a food-chain' isn't knowledge, it's words; and before it can become knowledge and give up its meaning, it would still need working on. The fact that we are using language all the time makes us forget that it is a code, and as teachers we tend to think we are transmitting knowledge directly when we tell someone something. This teacher didn't make that assumption: she avoided straightforward telling, and in doing so also avoided

the misapprehension that *because they had been told they knew.*
Before they could know, they had to work on it and make it over
into their own meanings: which is precisely what we see Mary
doing.

Even direct experience itself is not 'knowledge' in the way
Mary's generalization was. If – given rather unusual resources –
the teacher had arranged for her class to see a greenfly eating a
lettuce, a sparrow eating a greenfly, a cat eating a sparrow . . .
even then, the pupils would still have had to make the shift
from the separate events to the pattern and the abstract notion
of a chain. To grasp the relationships involved the pupils would,
again, have had to work upon it in something like the way they
do in this transcript. That knowledge is not inherent in the
experience, any more than it is in the diagram: it comes only
from exploring the experience in one particular way, which we
call biology.

III

The uttering of a high-powered generalization may signal a
moment of insight and recognition: 'Any acid added to any
carbonate makes carbon dioxide' said a third-year girl in a
chemistry lesson, suddenly understanding the experiments she
had been doing. It is this sort of realization that Polanyi (1973)
identifies when he writes:

> The change is irrevocable. A problem that I have once
> solved can no longer puzzle me; I cannot guess what I
> already know. Having made a discovery, I have become
> different; I have made myself into a person seeing and
> thinking differently. I have crossed a gap, the heuristic gap
> which lies between problem and discovery.

Where there is this sense of 'crossing the gap', one can apparently
identify a point where learning has been achieved.

But generalizations are not always acquired as sudden insights. More often the process is gradual. Moreover, generalizations are not all of one kind, nor are they all learnt in school.
Our pupils have been making generalizations of their own from
their earliest years: 'pimples come on your arms when you're
cold', said a four-year-old boy. Piaget made the distinction
between those concepts that children make by their own mental
efforts and those that were decisively influenced by adults: he
designates the first group as *spontaneous* and the second as

non-spontaneous (Vygotsky 1962). Vygotsky explored the matter further, and identified the crucial difference between them: 'The . . . inception of a spontaneous concept can usually be traced to a face-to-face meeting with a concrete situation, while a scientific concept involves from the first a 'mediated' attitude towards its object.'

Whereas children make their spontaneous concepts for themselves, by reflecting on their experiences, the generalizations they acquire through formal education are often, in the first place, presented to them in the form of new words or statements.

Notions like 'trade' or 'osmosis' have to be offered by adults, because they are highly complex concepts which are unlikely to be spontaneously discovered. They imply knowledge of a large number of separate phenomena which are only given a class-name once they have been identified as being part of a system which needs a conceptual label. And indeed, as Vygotsky comments, 'the *absence of a system* is the cardinal psychological difference distinguishing spontaneous from spontaneous concepts'.

In other words, children derive spontaneous generalized concepts from direct experience – bricks sink, wood floats – but they are not able, apparently, to organize the separate generalizations into a *system* which covers sinking and floating in general. Unlike those generalizations which are instantly grasped, scientific concepts come to mean more only as further experiences are identified as instances of them. Thus, Mary and Barney were initially presented with the abstraction 'food-chain'; then they considered actual phenomena within their experience. But consideration of their experience wasn't through direct observation in a face-to-face meeting: it was mediated by the abstraction 'food-chain' which helped them to interpret their experience. Thus, their experience was reorganized and given new meaning because they were now considering it in the light of the abstraction. Experience and abstraction reciprocally illuminated and explained each other. However, unless their spontaneous understanding of the way animals feed had already attained a certain degree of organization, they would not have been able to understand the scientific concept:

> The development of a spontaneous concept must have reached a certain level for the child to be able to absorb a related scientific concept. . . . Scientific concepts in turn

> supply structures for the upward development of the child's
> spontaneous concepts towards consciousness and deliberate
> use. (Vygotsky p. 109)

The nature of this interaction between spontaneous concepts created by direct experience and the power that scientific concepts can offer is best explored in relation to a practical situation.

IV

To illustrate how school knowledge is a different matter from everyday knowledge, let us consider a piece of the real world: a particular tract of the countryside with all the lives and activities, processes and occurrences that take place within it. Imagine a family who have a holiday cottage there to which they return every year. They have been coming a long time and have spent many hours talking to the local inhabitants, so they have an extensive knowledge of the place, and many memories. What they have learnt they have learnt by direct experience, or from the experience of others related to them by anecdotes. For the children, the place is gradually filling with meaning in the same way; to arrive at the same sort of knowledge, they have to go through the same sort of process – spending time here, living in the village, listening to the stories. What they will end up with is what for convenience we can call everyday knowledge.

But there is other knowledge than the everyday knowledge gained from having lived here. Our holiday-makers can transform the way the scene looks to them if they look through the frame of reference of one of the other sorts of knowledge they possess. For instance, they can consider it through the frame of reference of history, and what they see then is suffused with a particular awareness, that this is the late twentieth century and not the nineteenth or fourteenth, with all that that knowledge implies. The landscape and the lives and processes occurring in it are no longer simply things that happen to be going on, with personal associations for them, but are now perceived as outcomes. They think of the Viking invaders in this part of Wales, and the fact that they settled and lived here; they think of the tension between this picturesque village and its coal-mining past; they think of the local Lord, still owner of much of the area, whose forbear was hunted out of the valleys and across the mountains to this place in the last century, pursued by his miners, driven as they were beyond endurance.

The reality out there remains the same, but the perspective of history transforms the way it presents itself to the observers. They know something of how the Vikings lived on this land; yet they were never specifically taught that. What they learned in school, and from reading since, was how Vikings lived in general, and in particular at one or two sites where their remains have survived. Not here, though. They have taken their general knowledge, those separate propositions acquired outside this context, and applied it here so that now they *know* things about here that they never *learned* about here. And they can change their frame of reference, and interpret that identical scene in other ways completely. If they become physicists for a moment, the features of the scene are now the gull's wing-beat, the solar energy falling on that patch of ground, the generator in the next field.

Unlike the knowledge of the food-chains as it was presented to the biology class, this bit of reality doesn't come coded. But it evidently doesn't come as raw reality either, offering itself directly to the observers. In itself, it doesn't come as anything. What it does come as depends on the framework the observers choose to use. The very features of the scene that they find to be there, far from being 'given' as a basis on which they can impose patterns, are themselves determined by whether they're being ecologist, sociologist, geographer, ornithologist, linguist or economist.

These realities, the ones that are shown up under the lights of the different disciplines, are not ones that the visitors' children will acquire simply by being brought to the place and listening to the local tales. For them to see what the historians, economists and so on see, they would have to share the knowledge which those experts bring to bear on the scene, knowledge acquired elsewhere and in other ways, and formulated in particular propositions, and in patterns and groupings of propositions. It is all the same world that we live in, but one sees a landscape through the eyes of a historian when one sees the things in it as elements in the patterns of that discipline. To see them in the same way children would need to know the patterns, which would mean being aware of elements derived from many areas which would be impossible for them to know by direct, first-hand experience.

Moffett (1968) points out how features of our surroundings

are always given selective attention – 'we can never abstract all the features of our surroundings', he remarks, and points out that at any one time we select from the total experience around us those features which strike us as being relevant. But the criteria by which we judge what is relevant may sometimes derive from systems of ideas which we have previously built up; and he shows how, as we become more confident in handling concepts, we are able to synthesize fresh observations into these existing systems: 'The features are not only selected but *reorganised* and . . . *integrated with previously abstracted information.*' Features of our surroundings, that is, become at the same time examples of something more general.

Thus, to learn about this landscape in a historical way, the learner would have to work on the reality which presents itself, abstracting features from it by consciously applying classifications which are themselves abstractions, drawn from what he or she knows from elsewhere about Vikings, or nineteenth-century rural life, or ecclesiastical architecture. Only by making these associations can a learner make the scene express its historical meaning. But at the same time what is known about this specific place can modify the general knowledge one carries around and change generalizations: so the squires didn't invariably hold the countryside in such a secure grip – evidently a group of independent miners could send one packing permanently.

Knowledge proves its value when it is used. Indeed, unless it is used, it is inert and valueless. But the prevalent idea that we store up our knowledge while it's plentifully available – in school – and draw on it later, is an oversimplification, because the knowledge is learned by being used. Each time we apply a concept or generalization or fact, it acquires more meaning from the context it has been used in. Thus a generalization which might begin as an abstract schema, eventually comes to be felt as an aspect of the world: what was a mechanical application of the label 'food-chain' became for Mary and Barney something whose existence and effects they could perceive. By applying general knowledge about the Vikings to this settlement in Pembrokeshire, the knowledge is brought to life and increases in significance each time it is used. Knowledge not only proves its value in use: it *acquires* value by being used, and by having its application verified.

Seeing when the knowledge can be used is as much a part of learning as the original acquisition was. In order to know when to apply a concept or generalization to a new instance, we first need to know that this is the sort of case covered by the concept. It is possible to possess knowledge in some formal sense, and yet to be unable to operate it, because we do not discern its relevance to particular situations. One of the main ways we learn to do this is by exploring the implications of the instance, testing it against concepts we have, until we find ones that do fit. This is a process that we carry out, like Mary and Barney, mainly in talk.

School knowledge, as we have called it, is not the only sort of knowledge, nor is it always the most important. We have tried in this chapter to suggest the nature of its particular potency: it can provide ideas that sum up and pattern features of innumerable individual instances. Generalizations or conceptual terms like 'energy', 'feudal' or 'trade' represent complex abstractions which give control over thought. It is often assumed that coping with concepts like these is not only demanding intellectually, but is beyond many of our pupils. But it is not only well within the grasp of the majority, it is the only kind of learning that can convince many of them that school knowledge is worth bothering with. The remainder of this book addresses itself to the question of how it can be made generally available, and illustrates children of all kinds demonstrating their understandings.

Learning

I

We've said enough to show that the acquisition of school subject-knowledge, with its webs of general and specific facts, complex and diversely-drawn, is no simple matter. It is perhaps not surprising that large numbers of students fail to get far into it. Certainly, as a group, teachers are not in the habit of expressing surprise at the high order of failure they experience – we seem almost to expect it.

It is not for want of effort on our part that our students still so often fail to learn. It is despite the best efforts of serious teachers to improve their teaching that the semi-involvement and the half-baked understanding persist: still the knowledge doesn't get across; the students don't remember it, and cannot apply it to different contexts, and so on. It is as though there were a thick glass screen between us, and all our antics and sincerity on this side of the glass were ineffective. No wonder that so many – teachers and students – have reached the conclusion that serious academic knowledge is too complicated and intractable for the majority.

But there are other ways of looking at it all. Hitherto, our attempts to improve achievement have largely consisted, as we said above, of attempts to improve teaching – the ways in which we present the knowledge. This emphasis is natural enough since subject-knowledge comes to children almost exclusively as presented by us. We tell them the knowledge in person or through the books we provide. Even field-trips and laboratory experiments, which appear to be direct experience, are stage-managed by teachers: the experience is selected by us, and has meaning only through the concepts and ideas we supply. So the quality of the presentation can appear to be the critical factor; yet we seem to have exhausted the possibilities at that end, to no avail. But what if we shift our attention from what we do as teachers to what the learners do? That is what we propose, and what many teachers are now learning to do for themselves. Creative energy which formerly went into devising new and more efficient ways of presenting materials is being turned with profit towards understanding what pupils actually do when they encounter, mull over and try to express new ideas and information. These are the observable processes, accessible to us largely through listening to what the pupils say and reading what they write; through attending, in other words, to children's language.

We are not at the stage in our understanding where we can specify all the things learners need to do in order to engage with a presentation of knowledge and take it over as their own. But listening to tapes of students' conversations and studying the writing they do under different circumstances has already taught us something. There are certain sorts of processes, we can say, which apparently need to go on. If they don't, learning doesn't. Indeed, as far as we can see, they are what learning is – there isn't some separate event, more worthy of the name, which brings about the state of affairs we call knowledge. In this chapter we hope to point to some of these essential learning processes. Later we shall be considering how we can help them to occur.

II

There is a character in Roman history called Crassus. Let's suppose I have indicated to you in a few sentences who Crassus was and what he did. I can now claim with some appearance of justification that now you, the reader, know who Crassus is. And up to a point this would be true. You are in a position to make sense, at one level, of references to Crassus in books you may go on to read. You can avoid mistaking him for someone else, and can associate with his name one or two attributes I've supplied you with – 'He's the one who did X'. But it is also undeniable that your knowledge is of a different order from mine. I've come across him innumerable times and in varied contexts. There's a fullness and roundedness about my knowledge of Crassus that you don't share.

As a teacher, I'm in danger of forgetting what a difference this makes. I may expect a statement about Crassus, encountered in a text, to be as satisfying to you as to me, since we're both able to identify the character referred to. But my rich knowledge of Crassus makes me alert to new information in quite a different way: I'm responding with thoughts like 'That fits what I know from so-and-so – just what I'd have expected' or 'That explains so-and-so' or 'I just don't believe that'. Thus it's what I bring to the statement as much as what is in it that makes it a significant one for me, while for you, logical and well constructed though it may be, it brings about no potent new connections in your mind. It appears that all that other stuff that I know, even when it is not obviously relevant, somehow helps me to make sense of new knowledge that I meet.

Thus, an adequate response to a statement involves, it seems, a full sense of the individual items referred to. We suggested in the last chapter that pupils' learning gains power when they understand the patterns that knowledge makes, that these 'patterns' are represented by generalizations, and that school is in business to teach an awareness of these generalizations. But it begins to appear that before we can adequately relate to the generalized statement, we need as full a grasp as possible of the details that are its elements. The better the elements are known, the more meaning the generalization will carry. And knowing the elements includes knowing them in ways that are not immediately relevant to the sort of constructions that the subjects want to build on them.

For the purposes of teaching a discipline, pupils are often required to register only certain features of complex realities, and to ignore the rest as 'noise'. ('Anyway, can we get on?') The dogfish pinned out on the bench is there to establish in the pupils a knowledge of the internal organs and their arrangement. But the dogfish, far from presenting itself to the child as a concrete embodiment of an abstract diagram of organs, is screaming a multiplicity of other messages. It stinks; it is fascinating and repulsive. It is dead. It was once living and actually swam in the sea: which sea? where? It is what they eat in fish and chips in London, God help them – 'rock salmon' they call it. It would be good to shove in Susan's face. Where the edge of the specimen has folded inwards slightly so that the outside skin with its scales forms a border for the mauvish flesh, makes an interesting contrast of textures – good to paint, etc.

For attention to be concentrated on one highly specific aspect of a phenomenon, distractions from all the other aspects of it, which may in themselves be more immediately compelling, need to have died down. Perhaps that only happens when these (to the teacher) peripheral matters have received the full attention the learners want to give them. In any case, how else than by considering every aspect can the learners arrive for themselves at the teacher's, or the discipline's, notion of what is relevant? The questions that students spontaneously ask for themselves about a subject are different from those which the subject asks; but it is only by feeling that the subject's questions are real and worth answering that students can learn to see some features of a phenomenon as foreground and therefore relevant, and others as background and less relevant.

The first sort of process, then, which we can say appears to be an essential component of learning, is the process of taking full cognizance of the realities involved: getting to know the elements, registering what is there, familiarizing oneself with all aspects, handling them in different ways, looking at them under different lights, playing about with them. It's largely a matter of dwelling on the reality in different ways until one feels at home with it. It's a stage that may take some time – but which it would be a false economy to omit.

When we see what children do who have the opportunity to perform this handling process for themselves, we find the operation taking different forms. Here are two examples which happen to be in writing. Both are by eleven-year-old pupils on a World Studies course. The first is by one boy expressing his reactions to encountering the idea of 'Tundra' for the first time, but not by writing definitions or 'notes': after he'd written this piece, he made a tape of it, with sound effects and improvised music.

The Tundra

Dark cold		silence nothing
Jagged foamy		non fertile
ice sheet		wall of ice
nothing	nothing	nothing
cold	cold	cold
Frost bite		freeze froze
slippery clean		foamy solid
birds animals		going south
Nothing	Nothing	Nothing
Cold am I		cold
plants little		surviving
blizzards		ice bergs
	begging	
glaciers		slow rivers
death freeze		death
	The Tundra	

The second piece, by two boys working together, is a kind of running commentary on the rocks they are looking at.

1 The rock we are studying is called galena lead ore. It is quite heavy for its size. It has got lead which glitters when you move it. The colours are grey white and yellow. It is covered in little holes. It weighs about 1 lb. 4 ozs. It feels like sandpaper when you rub it quite hard.

2 This rock is the second rock we are studying. The name of the rock is pegmatite, you can get it at Portleven in Cornwall. It weighs in metric metres 430 grams. It has a small quantity of crystal along the surface. Some parts of it glitter, it has long black strips which in fact are long crystals of a mineral which I don't know.

3 The third rock we are studying is called pumice. It is very light because a lot of air is getting inside because there are thousands of little holes. It weighs 80 grammes and you use it to get hard skin off your feet. It feels like a bone and looks like a thing from some one's inside of their leg. The colour is sort of grey and brown.

4 This rock is called copper pyrites. It is very shiny and has little stones imbedded in it. One is called quartz. This one like the first one feels like sandpaper.

And here it is happening in talk. Although a teacher is helping things along, what the fifteen-year-old student is doing for himself exactly fits the account we gave – registering what is there, familiarizing oneself with all aspects. He even provides us with a nicely identifiable affective response. In this case, although the object is familiar enough, 'what is there' is something quite new to the pupil, and in learning to see the new features he is learning to see as a biologist.

Teacher What's happening now?
Pupil It's crinkling up because its longitudinal muscles come together –
Teacher Good.
Pupil – and they're making the outer ones push out and that makes it move – and it puts its – what do you call it?
Teacher It's all right you can say wrinkles. Now watch this bit. Now just that bit just that bit there. What muscles have contracted to make it long and thin?

Pupil	The long – the longitudinal muscles.
Teacher	No the longitudinal ones are like this – when they shortened –
Pupil	Oh the outer ones come out and the circular ones come out.
Teacher	Now let's do it again
Pupil	Ah look they're squashed together now because the longitudinal ones have gone in like and then – it's going to stretch now
Teacher	That's it. Which ones have contracted to make it stretch?
Pupil	The circular ones – look if you're looking you can actually see them
Teacher	Yes that's right
Pupil	It's a good worm (*affectionately*)
Teacher	Now I want you to tell me now why when it stretches out why does it stay in its new position. What anchors it to its new position?
Pupil	It's the – what're they called again – you know
Teacher	You try
Pupil	(*looking in book*) Tell you when I find it – caters, bristles
Teacher	Chaetae
Pupil	Chaetae
Teacher	Chaetae
Pupil	Chaetae

He has to work through and almost unlearn his everyday knowledge about worms in order to see it as a biologist does, and thereby perceive new things in it. The actual components of this bit of reality weren't there for him at all until he learnt to see them at the same time as he learnt the biologist's terms: now he has to 'register what's there', take full account of it, become fully aware of it by watching it, living with it, soaking himself in the experience, recapitulating what he sees. His words seem to help to direct his perception, and he repeats the names both to establish them and to confirm his consciousness of the new *things* he has discovered. As the familiar worm becomes strange for him, the excitement shows him why it's worth bothering with biology.

III

Concrete realities encountered in the laboratory, bits of rock that can be passed round, the details of the story of 1066, accounts of how the Aztecs dressed, ate and treated their prisoners, these may be matter for extended handling and mulling over, but can't be said to present problems of understanding. The pupil doesn't mutter 'This is hard' while watching a film of a volcano erupting.

But students do not only meet phenomena, real or represented, in school. They also have to cope with ideas, abstractions, terms, generalizations, explanations and so forth, and these are much more important. Feeling secure with the particular realities they rest on is, as we've seen, an important condition for coping, and there are things children can do to get to this state; but then there are other processes, rather different in kind. Eleven-year-olds again:

Phil   We depend on
Andrew   the sun, rain, man working and animals ploughing it up, fertilizer to make the soil rich again, then er insecticides to kill most of the insects and pests
Phil   mostly sun and rain and fertilizer
Andrew   and before, all it depended on, in the middle ages and early on, were t'sun and t'rain
Phil   Plants grew then, got eaten by animals . . . droppings, humus came out o' t'plants and dropped
Andrew   plants died
Phil   eaten by animals and then t'animals died
Andrew   that'd be man as well, 'cause man did bury his men then, isn't it, that all goes back into the soil, but nowadays there's
Paul   fertilizers
Andrew   plants grow, plants are eaten by animals, plants are eaten by animals, some plants are eaten by men, vegetables and that, man eats animals so they don't go, die into the ground really, and man's droppings go down to t'sewers into t'sea and pollute that, so all of it's really wasted

They've read an extract about the soil, explaining the cycle of life and death which keeps it fertile in nature and the way modern techniques disrupt the cycle. Here the lads seem to be going over the ideas for themselves, trying them out to see if they fit, confirming for each other that they've got them – what we might call 'rehearsing'. It seems one of the most obvious ways to master an explanation in a text, one we all resort to – in our heads at any rate.

But are there other ways of engaging with an argument, other than by going over it for oneself? One way is by throwing in a spanner. The next contribution is from Paul, previously silent apart from one word:

Paul   Ah, but now of course we have tractors, don't we
Andrew   Yes but they're not doing much good are they
Paul   They are
Andrew   The old ways are best

'The old ways are best' is what the text implied, or appeared to. Paul challenged this. But, typically, this issue is not pursued at this point; instead they preoccupy themselves with an 'irrelevant' aspect of the matter and argue about how much a tractor can plough in a day. (This is 'handling the elements' in the way we referred to earlier.) Phil stops this one with hard knowledge:

Phil   Er, 25, 25 acres takes about a day even with a tractor 'cause I've been on a tractor with somebody

Then they return to the theme, but this time they are not repeating the argument of the text but drawing implications from it:

Andrew   In t'olden days though they were just small fields but nowadays they're all right big and it's getting blown away is all t'soil, isn't it, all t'soil's getting blown away and it's right hot and dusty
Paul   It'll soon become a desert
Andrew   Yes that's what's happening. If we're not careful it'll all, we'll all become a desert

Rehearsing, putting counter-examples, dwelling on one singled-out minor element of the topic, bringing in other knowledge not derived from the text, speculating about implications: only the first of these accords more or less with the traditional idea of what it means to learn. Yet repeatedly in transcripts like this one we find pupils engaging in all the others, and are compelled to conclude that they are inseparable from the ostensibly central process of 'taking in' the knowledge itself in the form in which it is presented.

This is only what we would expect. Consider, for instance, what must necessarily be involved for a concept like 'erosion' to get learnt. Teaching would take the student a good part of the way: typically, it would consist of the provision of a definition and of illustration. A teacher might show a film of a small fall of rock and dust from a cliff on a stormy day; but this would not be enough – the pupil might get the impression that erosion was exposure to wind, or material falling into the sea, or the uncovering of a clean rock surface. But if the film also showed a hillside grazed bare and worn down by goats, streams carrying bits of rock down mountains, and a then-and-now map showing a coastline which has receded, then the pupil's chance of 'getting' the concept would be greater. But more would still need to be done, this time by the student rather than the teacher, before the idea could be regarded as securely established. Students might take the partial concept of erosion and apply it to phenomena they were personally familiar with, appealing to the teacher or each other for feedback – 'Is this an example of erosion? and this?' They might speculate and hypothesize – what would be the outcome of the felling of trees on a steep hillside, the diverting of a stream into a new channel, the removal of a stone jetty, or the impeding of a river's flow by weed-growth? The concept 'erosion' as used by geographers means more than the everyday term 'wearing away', because it includes the idea that the material is removed and eventually deposited somewhere else. If students are able to use the concept to mediate their everyday observations, it will help them firstly to notice that material *is* removed, and then to ask where it goes to. Thus, they will begin to make predictions which will guide their discoveries. It is not in concentrating on the definition of the concept or the stated version of the knowledge, in an attempt to impress it on the mind, that the concept or knowledge effectively gets learnt, but in the knockabout between the new ideas and the knowledge and experience they get brought up against.

What pupils say and write can be particularly revealing at the stage when a new idea has been encountered but not yet completely married into the student's existing system of ideas; it is at this point that the perceptive teacher can find the clues which will enable him or her to help clear remaining obstacles out of the way.

Teacher   Okay now you're going to classify the various things

on that picture into one of the three groups, which
are – Karen?

Pupil 1 Living, once living and er
Pupil 2 Never lived
Teacher Yes, living, once living, and never-lived. Right off
you go.

* * *

Pupil 3 Sir – sir –
Teacher Mmm?
Pupil 3 Sir are clouds living?
Teacher – er – well what do you think?
Pupil 3 I think they're not, but Julie says they are
Teacher Oh. Why do you think they're living, Julie?
Pupil 4 Well, they move, and sort of grow and die and that
Teacher Ye–es. What else have you argued about – anything?
Pupil 5 Is wind living?

Or again: 'A car explodes as it goes along the road. This is
because of the way the engine works. A spark explodes inside
the engine and the car blows up.' (ten-year-old boy)

The twelve-year-old pupils doing science knew well enough
that clouds and wind aren't alive in the way that people and
animals are (and, by the way, 'animals' is another term that
causes problems: animals are furry and have four legs – why is
the biology teacher calling this worm an animal?). The confusion
arises because the already-held meaning of 'living' is being
called into question by the work on classification that is going on,
and there is a complicated process of testing out meanings under
way. They know 'living things' in the way most of us do: by
having slowly acquired the concept as a label for things like
plants and animals. But the teacher's 'living' is a scientific
concept: in other words, you apply it according to strictly defined
criteria. The only way to learn such a concept is to try it out on
cases and see if it fits: or, simply, to memorize it and hope that
some day it will make sense. But the teacher in this case didn't
simply 'train' them to use the concept; he asked them to
identify the characteristics they felt that living things possessed,
and then test against their lists the things they were having
problems with – wind, clouds, fire, mud, water. So rather than
insisting that they took over his definition, he encouraged them

31

to build and refine their own, and the process of locating in their own knowledge of the world the features that contribute to a concept of 'living' was one that was done collaboratively and successfully. After that process, the strengths of the scientists' definition would be likely to be appreciated.

The ten-year-old boy, unfortunately, didn't get that opportunity. The exploding car was the outcome of the associations which the word 'explosion' had for him. The teacher had used the word in an unfamiliar way to refer to a controlled and harnessed phenomenon. So although he knows that cars don't explode as they go along the road, with a kind of intellectual shrug of resignation, he makes what sense he can of what he thinks he's been told.

We have now identified two processes as being part of learning. Traditionally, they have both been regarded as at best incidental, at worst distracting and misleading. The first was 'handling the elements', the detail of the phenomena that the subject knowledge is about: it involves getting to know them in all their aspects, both what is obviously relevant and what seems ostensibly irrelevant. It involves, too, not only an intellectual comprehension of them but also seeing how they affect the feelings in general. The second process was 'handling the generalizations and ideas', of putting them to work, applying them to different contexts, looking at existing knowledge under the new light they throw: all those activities of trying and testing which go beyond merely storing a verbal formulation of a fact. It remains for us to introduce a third mode of relating to knowledge, one which is perhaps the most vital of the three.

IV

Students might dutifully attempt to perform the processes we have outlined, directing their attention to this and that aspect of the material and discovering by active application of the new facts and ideas that there were implications for one's understanding of certain other areas. But they might still find that they could not answer for themselves the question, 'What has this got to do with me?' The whole area of study can still seem like something that remains at a distance from them, something they do because they are told to, not because they want to.

We suggest that arriving at a clear sense of 'why I'm choosing to get involved with this' is inseparable from the more obvious processes by which learners make knowledge their own. The comments of these two boys illustrate what is at stake:

> In my first lesson of Social Education I think it is going to be a very interesting course. I am not quite sure what to do on the question of ideas and civilization so that now I am going to try and find out more about this subject by going to the Library. In the meantime I have been thinking about Chapter 1 in the yellow book (the Ancient World). I wrote this when I paused during my thinking. I am just beginning to understand some of it, but some bits are puzzling.
>
> It is fascinating how the shape of man has developed. Before a few weeks ago when my sister told me about the skull of prehistoric ape man I had never heard of such things before. Now I am really beginning to catch on and like the subject. I am finding it difficult to concentrate because of noise and Henry Collins etc. I have now got some plain paper so that I can do drawings of the inside of caves and the heads of the Southern ape man up until the modern man. Civilization begins when men learn to live together in towns, villages and cities etc. I wrote this in so that I may remember it for later.
>
> (Stephen, 15, first entry in logbook)

Contrast:

> The earliest I can remember about learning English was in the first year at secondary school. In the first second and third year all we did was to write essays with funny headings. In these preliminary years we also learnt writing techniques and learnt a little about poetry.
>
> In the fourth and fifth year we were mainly taught exam techniques and what questions the examiners might ask. We also learnt one play (*Macbeth*) and two books (*The day of the Triffids* and *The golden apples of the sun*). Both were science fiction books. The main concern we learnt was concerned with the exam. I can't see how this type of English can be useful to me, because I have taken up a career in engineering.
>
> (First-year engineering apprentice)

The first lad had the chance to make his own sense of his

classroom experience: the second was treated as passive recipient, resented it, and was disaffected by it. It is what the first lad is getting that the second lad disastrously missed; and the final process we wish to draw attention to is the one by which the students help themselves to get it – that is, the things learners do to find a personal meaning and significance in what they are studying. We can see Stephen at it: by writing in this way he is not merely recording an affinity he already feels for the subject, he is working to bring it about. It is a function that we often find being performed by unpressured writing for a trusted audience. Teachers, in encouraging such writing by the provision of logbooks and other opportunities, are usually hoping to get thinking on paper about the subject – that is, all the processes of handling the topic, questioning, speculating and so on which we've already referred to – and sometimes they do. But some students use the writing for another purpose, namely for establishing a relationship with the enterprise as a whole, and for contemplating with satisfaction or surprise the idea of themselves as students of whatever it is. 'Here I am studying anthropology!' is the sort of message that comes over between the lines in this next piece:

Anthropologist in the Xingu
It is a very fascinating story, and I think he is lucky to be able to tell it. They could easily not have accepted him, and left him to die. It was very exciting for him I expect. I would like to be him, the waura tribe are very interesting. The Waura tribe know alot about medicens and stuff which we don't. We are ruled by machines, they do everything for us. But the waura are opposite to us, they have to get their own food. And make everything which they use. They don't use money, so they don't fight over it. They seem to enjoy life alot without using machines, they eat all different things aswell. If you stayed their for a very long time you might not want to go back to civilastion. I think it would be good if people went to live their for a year, they would appreciate life better. And might even find it fun. The waura tribe must be clever to keep alive. Because if most of us went and tryed to live like them, not many people would keep alive.
(Carol, 13)

From the fact that when they get the chance so many students choose to use logbooks and similar channels for this sort of personal purpose, we are forced to conclude that the process is important and should be fostered. What's more, it's a fair hypothesis that students who are not involved at a satisfying level with what they are studying could possibly be helped by being provided with such a channel. It is a good example of the way in which our educational aims, our ideas of what we should be trying to do, may be best arrived at by analysing what pupils do rather than by armchair philosophizing.

Not infrequently, of course, it happens that a student hits it off with a topic at first sight. Sometimes we can, from the outside, see how the topic meshes in with a preoccupation we have already noted in the learner; more often, we can't explain the attraction, but assume that in some way the subject provides evidence relevant to deeply held personal projects, aims and desires in the student.

More often, though, our typical student starts from at the most a vague willingness to be interested and sometimes not even that. Becoming interested then seems to depend on finding things in the topic which bear on matters with which one is already in some way concerned; or perhaps on discovering that the information can – even if indirectly – provide answers to questions one has been wanting to ask. After all, information in itself is neither interesting nor uninteresting; it is the context which gives it significance. 'What is an ayatollah?' was transformed overnight in 1978 from quiz-programme trivia to burning issue. Unless the information is of intrinsic interest to the learner, he or she has to find a personal 'way in' to it, often by spinning a familiar context around it. Once the process of studying a topic gets under way in the first place, it can then become self-sustaining.

The more one gets into a topic the more one is likely to find connections with matters one is already interested in. Apparently alien facts are suddenly seen to be cases of a type familiar from existing knowledge or experience; or one may realize that if this obtains in this area, then something similar may be true of some more immediately and personally important matter. And often, to the teacher, when a pupil does see connections like these, it can be unexpected because the connections may not be visible to the teacher:

Biology teacher   Today we'll be looking at bacteria and viruses and –

35

Pupil   Miss! Did you see *Starsky and Hutch* on Saturday?

As it happens, *Starsky and Hutch* was about a man carrying a plague virus. Television, personal experience, what has been read or heard about – all this unorganized, apparently irrelevant accumulation of facts and impressions is the stuff out of which pupils build the contexts in which school knowledge can mean something.

There are plenty of opportunities to make connections between the familiar, warm, messy, already interesting world of experience and the cool and precise propositions of subject knowledge; but all too often they are wantonly disregarded. These fourteen-year-old girls are talking about biology:

Girl 1 Well, it's all boring, isn't it?
Girl 2 Yeah, well she always –
Girl 3 Yeah, but it shouldn't be, should it?
Girl 1 But it's all them long names and things and she
Girl 3 Everytime she starts a new topic, and she says 'This is all about' – oh like when we did reproduction and
All Yeah
Girl 3 And we all thought, gor this'll be interesting but
Girl 1 And it was just lists of things to learn
Girl 2 Remember when we did the blood? and I'd cut my finger at break and tried to show her and she didn't even look

If pupils are allowed to explore widely around the topics they are studying, some of the matters they will get onto will appear to the teacher to be unrelated and irrelevant. Sometimes they really will be that; more often they are attempts to link together the new material with existing preoccupations, to find the familiar in the unknown.

There are various ingenious techniques for getting students into some sort of initial engagement with a topic so that points of personal relevance have a chance of being found. (One of them, 'A–Z', is described in the chapter 'Contexts for language'.) But often all that is required is quite simply the *opportunity* for students to form a reaction to a topic and do a bit of freewheeling thinking around it. The expert ornithologist may be able to concentrate on the different flight-patterns of buzzard and sparrow-hawk; but the child, who does not know those birds in the rounded way the expert does, is concerned to know quite other things, and may not be capable of seeing the flight-pattern at all. More important may be what they look like, who in the class has seen them, which is the fiercest, the strongest, the rarest . . .

How do you feel about it? What thoughts and curiosities does it give rise to in you? It is surprising how little it takes to get this responsive and reflective process started, in talk or in writing. Most of us like to go on about things. An eleven-year-old class was asked those questions after reading a colour-supplement piece about the recent discovery of a stone-age tribe, the Tasaday, in a remote part of New Guinea. There was some chat, then they wrote.

My thoughts about the discovery of the tuesday
I think if anybody who found the tuesday tribe it would be a big shock our world I think will be better than the world of the tuesday tribe. I wish I was the one who found the tribe they would poropley kill me so I couldent tell about there secrecy But I would not like to just eat fish and smaller animals may be they are scared of bigger animals it must be very unpleasant not to ware clothes or just sleep on cold and damp floors, there is onley fragments of wood to sit on and stone the tuesday tribe are superbly fit there is onley one way they get diseses and thats by other people and if they do get dises they would die the children are teached by there mothers to read and write but they do not go to school if maybe they were to go out of there secret world they would be killed or hanged but is very rearly they go out of there secret place we dont know write were they live but they might live in caves or open grounds. Maybe if they did find and kill bigger animals they would not be frightened now more or else they might have a god nowed by animal which must never be killed I think they are never fighting together they are always pecfull some of the tribe well all over the tribe is religious because of ther God of animals if someone was merded maybe they would have a court or a jung to find the killer maybe if they found the killer they would maybe hanged.

With all its misconceptions, this is not a bad basis for further

37

enquiry: the student has got into a relationship with the topic and established an interest in all sorts of aspects of it; a teacher would have no difficulty in knowing how to take him on from here.

So the motivation to get into an area of knowledge can come precisely from getting into it, and finding that there are things which have to do with existing interests. But there is a different force which may carry students along, namely their enjoyment of the *processes* of learning, almost irrespective of the content. That is to say, students can discover the pleasures of talking together, and of particular kinds of writing and reading. If these are allowed and encouraged to occur in the active, open (and time-consuming) forms we've been describing, with full scope for handling ideas, following up associations, drawing personal conclusions and so on, then the business is likely to be inherently satisfying. The engagement of the learners, in the examples quoted, is at least as much with their own intellectual skills and with the potentialities of thinking together in a group as with the knowledge under consideration. We know from our own experience that thinking something through, perhaps on paper, can be its own reward, that conversation can be satisfying in itself quite apart from the deposits of new knowledge it leaves us with, and that once one has experienced collaborative problem-solving one wants to do more of it. It is a basic task of teaching to create climates and environments in which these activities can go on. An important part of our argument is that these processes, which we are advocating as means towards the fuller acquisition of understanding, are themselves powerful motivators of learning.

V

The need for these active processes of learning rests in the end on the fundamental fact that we cannot strictly speaking be given knowledge but have to make it for ourselves. Knowledge is a state of our heads; what can be presented to us is words, symbols, representations or real things; these are not knowledge but the clues, starters or signposts on the basis of which we *make* our knowledge, come to realizations and form ideas. Just as we have to do our seeing for ourselves, so no one else can give us a knowing of something.

Generally, of course, the processes go on in people's heads. They are covered by our notion of 'thinking'. In this form they are difficult to observe because what goes on is invisible, below the surface. But, as we've already seen, the processes can also be manifested above ground, so to speak; or at least something which commonly goes on above the surface appears to be intimately associated with them, namely language. Language passing between people can evidently serve as a medium in which elements can be played about with, abstractions tried out, implications drawn and attitudes formulated; people seem to perform these essential operations not only on their own but with each other, in talk and in writing. Thus the processes can be either between people or within the individual: interpersonal or intrapersonal.

This is a fact of great educational significance. We have no access to processes inside the head, but *inter*personal transactions are open and visible, and their operations are thus susceptible to our influence. This is why the possibility arises of affecting the quality of the learning process as it occurs. We can now entertain a hope that what occurs in one way for the few with apparent spontaneity (in the head, for the successful academic learner) may be induced to occur, to equal effect, in the other way – in overt speech and writing – for the many. Perhaps what some think we can get others to say.

Moreover, it is not only in the interpersonal mode that language is crucial. The form that thinking takes inside the head is more of a mystery, but there is no doubt that language plays a significant part in it. One thing that is known about language is that what at one stage happens openly in speech, at a later stage happens internally as thought (Vygotsky 1962, Piaget 1959); so there is reason to expect that by improving the quality of the interpersonal language of children, we may thereby be assisting the development of thought. The idea that speech and writing are preceded by thought, and that the language act is the product of thought and learning is only partially true: it seems also true that talking and writing *generate* thoughts and learning. This is the general point of view that underlies everything else in this book.

Language

I

Talkers need listeners, writers need readers. In school, the talkers certainly have their listeners: the teachers do most of the talking (Bellack *et al.* 1966) and they have a captive audience. When it's the students' turn to have the floor, it is as writers that they have it: teachers rarely write. But do the students have readers? Not in the usual sense, for teachers are not like other readers: they don't want to be entertained or instructed or interested or personally involved. They read instead, apparently, in order to proofread and correct errors, to award marks or grades, and to make sure that the pupils were paying attention in class. How else to account for the kinds of response they make? (See Dunsbee and Ford 1980)

As long as the language transactions take those forms, then we stand to learn little about what we need to know about – our students' learning processes. If the students' language is to offer access to their thinking, then the right sort of language must be occurring, and then we need to be attentive to it in the right way. We will have to allow them to talk, and learn ourselves to be hospitable listeners; we must read as real readers, responding to the voice which is addressing us; and the writing will need to exhibit the thinking we are interested in and not merely reflect back received knowledge.

It is not easy in the hurly-burly of teaching to listen attentively and read sympathetically. It takes time, which may have to come from things that seem more important like preparation and marking, or, in the classroom, ensuring that everyone is 'getting on'. It may seem a more efficient use of our energies to get round and 'help' as many as possible, telling them what they need to know, getting them on to the next stage. Moreover, it can often seem, on first listening to tapes or reading pupils' writing in a responsive way, that what's there isn't worth giving up valuable time for. What often seems to emerge is a shapeless, clumsy, incoherent mass of irrelevancies, incorrectnesses and ignorance. Is this what we are supposed to see as evidence of learning? Our feeling may be confirmed that our pupils will get the best value out of us from what we can give them, not from our allowing them to get in a mess for themselves.

But if we insist on giving them what they seem to need, devoting our efforts to telling them the knowledge in the best way we can and guiding them through carefully structured writing procedures which will yield an organized-looking statement of it, we do not keep them out of that mess. The mess is still there: the difference is that it does not show. But we *need* it to show, so that we can learn, by studying the errors, exactly what this particular pupil *does* understand, where she has difficulty, where he needs most help, and so on. Success depends not only on our teaching processes but on their learning processes – which are distinct operations that need to be provided for and are not simply automatically created by teaching. It is in this unpromising material that the means lie, in the long run, of helping them far more.

First impressions may be disheartening but are unlikely to persist. The habit of attentive listening and reading will be found to be self-reinforcing, because in making ourselves a receptive audience we do not merely gain access to what is going on: we change it. In taking what they have to say seriously, we confer a new dimension on the relationship, to which they typically respond by opening up and allowing unexpected qualities to surface. Those opportunities for language which best help us, by enabling the learning processes to see the light of day, are also the ones which help them to learn, and to find satisfaction in learning. Something as apparently small as providing a tape-recorder to preserve students' efforts may signal to them that their teacher values what they do and say; but both the feeling of being valued, and the uses to which those tapes can be put radically affect the quality of what takes place.

The hybrid nature of language is the key to understanding this. The satisfactions we derive from producing it effectively are on two quite different planes. Our words give expression to our thoughts, ideas, perceptions and so on, allowing us to be conscious of them in a new way; but they also communicate and make contact with other people, affecting them and perhaps leading them to respond. Educationally, it is the first aspect, the thinking that language can carry that we are primarily interested in – the content of the words used in the attempt to understand something; but the speakers and writers themselves need the sense of getting through to somebody, even when they may in fact be sorting their ideas out for their own benefit; if we speak to unresponsive or hostile faces, we dry up. Since children's experience of using language is largely in face-to-face communication, their need for a real 'audience' when they write is greater than it may be with adults, who have learnt to write for themselves or for some unspecified 'readers in general'. If they are to talk, and hopefully advance their understanding by talking, they will need what they feel to be real talking situations – which means as a rule informal conversation rather than exchanges in a large group in highly constrained circumstances. By listening and reading in the attentive way we need to for *our* purposes, we become the audience they will feel able to talk and write openly for. Even when they talk to each other, our role may be important as a second-line audience, as licensed eavesdroppers via the tape-recorder. We can confirm for them the value of talking, with the result that they come to see it as a serious educational activity, become conscious of their own performance in it and take an interest in improving, especially if we let them replay the tape and read the transcripts. The students can also, of course, be the audience for each other's writing.

If we are prepared to encourage conversation between groups of friends in our classrooms, the talk will be of the type which one finds in conversations, and we should be prepared for this. It will not look like an orderly march towards understanding; it will not replicate the exchanges between teacher and pupils that are typical of the normal lesson. We may at first feel uncomfortable with a form of linguistic behaviour which is so unlike the single-minded pursuit which is the image most of us have of learning. But the language, and the social uses of it, which the students bring to school with them are the only ones they have: we have no choice but to work with them. Certainly we may influence them as time goes on, extending and modifying where they fall short of what classroom learning demands; but we cannot kit them out with a complete new language and style of behaviour as they come in through the classroom door. Our interest as teachers is in furthering learning, not in producing speakers who are more respectably turned out. The language for learning *must* be in the first place the speaker's own familiar language; after all, we are asking it to perform the function of thinking, and it will need to come as easily and naturally as thought; that is why it needs to be the language which the students wear as close to them as their skin.

Teachers may say that they already give children scope to use their own language; but by tightly framing the slots the language is to go in (by the type of questions, the space or time left for the answer, the 'structure' of the paragraph-headings) they may in fact deny children the opportunity to employ their habitual language strategies: that is, to come at it their own way, to make their own links with the context, and to express their personal stake in their statements. 'Using your own language' means that you use your own words to say the things you want to. When somebody else tries to decide for you when and how you will express yourself, then what you produce is 'your own language' only in a watered-down sense.

The other reason for showing hospitality towards students' own language is that the features which we find distracting or irritating at a first encounter may be more functional than they seem. What we notice immediately when we start listening to tapes is the irrelevancies. Here, for instance, is a snatch of talk in a fifth-year history class, where four girls are supposed to be talking about the 1914–18 war. The discussion has been serious:

June	You can't really say we won the First World War, can you?
Gill	Yes but we didn't lose
Kath	But we didn't win, we lost just as many men as what the other sides did

But in the middle of it, this happens:

Gill	We had our new carpet laid down last night, it's lovely
June	Is it a new one?
Gill	Mmm
Kath	A new carpet? What colour?

One of the girls mentions that her family has a new Hoover ('new fashion model, cost £40'). Altogether, it sounds like the kind of 'discussion' that convinces teachers that such small group talk is too often purposeless, rambling and pointless.

But instead of being censorious, let's ask a different question: what is happening, and why is it happening? The answer can only be speculative, but it looks as though there is a process going on here that is perhaps typical of discussions. They have been talking seriously, and they will continue to talk seriously again. ('Let's discuss propaganda in the First World War' says one of them a minute and a half later, and they do.) But they know each other well, and the social dimensions of talk are as rich as the intellectual: June and Kath will want to know about Gill's new carpet, because they know her and her house. The agenda for talk is *always* a mixture of thought and feeling ('cognitive and affective') and the better the talkers know each other then the more easily the two intertwine. Moreover, at the moment, the girls are relaxing. The serious discussion has been momentarily displaced by 'chat', before the next surge of intensity. The girls themselves, listening to the tape of their talk later, said it was 'a kind of coffee break': 'we'd been working hard and we needed a rest'.

This feeling is familiar to everyone. It's a rare kind of talk which proceeds consistently on the level of serious and intense concentration without jokes, anecdotes, gossip or some other tension-reliever. Any tape of adults talking would show the same thing. But in school, it can be seen as off-the-point and inconsequential digression if the teacher isn't conscious that it is the natural pattern for talk when the participants are fully involved. These three talkers are discussing a poem they have read.

Jan　It's like people that pick out the lobsters and things they want and then have them cooked in restaurants. It's horrible that

Kim　Or even, you know, cook -er, pick out the fish

Cath　The fish swimming around in tanks – 'I'll have that one'

Jan　Yes – yes

Cath　Oh dear

Jan　Somebody was telling me about – oh, I know it's my friend's husband – his aunty in Ireland, they've got chickens, and, you know, they've got to go out and pick the one they're going to have for dinner sort of thing

Kim　Mmm

Cath　Well, they keep rabbits for that sort of thing

Jan　Yes, that's right

Cath　In France

Kim　Ugh

The three are in fact experienced teachers on an in-service course; but their talk still shows the same weaving in and out of serious and light, intense and casual, concentrated and digressive.

But are the digressions really so digressive? There is some reference in the poem which is not instantly clear to them, so here they are explaining it to themselves by indicating *familiar* experiences which are examples of the same sort of thing: these experiences, recounted to each other, fill out the meanings of the poem, and are themselves seen in a different way by being considered together as examples of that custom.

So we need to look a second time at features of children's language – or of *anybody's* language – that at first look like evidence of mere lack of direction. They may be a means of carrying out one of the essential processes; or they may be small indulgences of the sort which we all, if we're honest, find we need when we're thinking hard about something – coffee breaks.

II

To give the flavour of the sort of thing that emerges when we listen carefully to tapes, and of what ordinary students are capable of when someone is paying them attention, we now present three 'language events'. The first two demonstrate what children can do on their own without help: and the third raises the consequent question: when we do help, what do we achieve?

The Poison Tree

I was angry with my friend;
I told my wrath, my wrath did end.
I was angry with my foe;
I told it not, my wrath did grow.

And I water'd it in fears,
Night & morning with my tears;
And I sunned it with smiles,
And with soft deceitful wiles.

And it grew both day and night,
Till it bore an apple bright;
And my foe beheld it shine,
And he knew that it was mine.

45

And into my garden stole
When the night had veil'd the pole:
In the morning glad I see
My foe outstretch'd beneath the tree

Blake: *Songs of Experience*

The teacher has given the poem to the class of fourteen-year-olds, and asked them to discuss it in their normal small, working groups. Some of the groups have tape-recorders with them. They have never seen the poem before.

In this group, there are six students. They begin, as children so often do, by trying to sort out the specific meanings:

1	*Joan*	What does wrath mean?
2	*Shan*	What does wrath mean?
3	*James*	Anger

Their talk isn't simple and linear. It weaves together their understanding of bits and pieces, their grasp of the whole, their personal response, and anything in their heads that seems to help.

14	*Hugh*	You told – you told – not to be angry. I'm being angry; I'm being angry so I mustn't be angry. So he told his anger to stop
15	*Shan*	I don't think I like it
16	*James*	But you're not talking about a real tree, are you? It's a hypothetical tree
17	*All*	It's a what? a what?
18	*James*	Hypothetical
19	*Kate*	Is that like a hypotenuse?
20	*James*	Imaginary

Hugh begins with an attempt at elucidation, but Shan at the moment is confused: she 'doesn't think' she likes it. James wants it to be clear that the poem is talking about a 'hypothetical tree'; this is the way he has available to him at the moment of talking about symbolism.

Then there is a conflict:

22	*Shan*	Is it an apple tree?
23	*Marion*	Yes
24	*James*	No
25	*Marion*	Yes!
26	*James*	No!
27	*Joan*	'And it grew both day and night, Till it bore an apple bright; And my foe beheld it shine,'
28	*Shan*	And did someone steal the apple from the tree?

The pupils themselves sort out conflicts, but not at all in the way a teacher would. Joan's re-reading of the poem is something that a teacher might hesitate to do, but that the group constantly does: on four occasions in this brief snatch of talk a different person reads some or all of the poem. And Shan persists in asking questions – she asks seven altogether; asks them because she doesn't know the answers, and wants to, and by asking them, she becomes the pivot figure in the discussion (though this was probably not obvious to the group at the time): in the attempt to answer her questions, the group gets increasingly close to the centre of the poem.

If we follow Shan's questions through, we can see how in group talk of this kind a student can follow a preoccupation with the assistance and support of colleagues. She asks:

2   What does wrath mean?
10 Yes, but how . . . (an unfinished question)
22 Is it an apple tree?
28 And did someone steal the apple from the tree?
45 What does foe mean?
48 What does wiles mean? Like someone's wily?
57 Where's the apple?

And then, finally, makes two crucial pronouncements:

62 Maybe he took his anger out on somebody and killed them
65 I think it's quite good because the first time you read it you think he's talking about an apple tree, and you don't see what he's getting at . . .

Shan is determined to sort out basic meanings of words, but

not to the exclusion of the greater, more important meaning which is the whole poem.

Hugh, on the other hand, performs a completely different function in the group. He is closest to the role a teacher would take up, alternately gatekeeping, and summarizing, although he also asks questions. It is generally Hugh that works the group towards articulating its interpretations.

14   You told – you told – not to be angry. I'm being angry, I'm being angry so I mustn't be angry. So he told his anger to stop

He answers Shan's questions:

31   Yes, someone did try to steal it

And sometimes quizzes the others:

33   You think he's talking about feelings, do you?

But the most exciting thing about this transcript is the way the group successfully, collaboratively, begin to work out the interpretation of the poem. They do together, with mutual support, what none of them could have done individually; and they do in talk far more sophisticated and subtle things than they could yet do in writing.

38	*James*	I think it's about his erm anger with his friend
39	*Joan*	Do you think someone dies in it then?
40	*James*	It's not a natural tree he's talking about. Doesn't nick an apple and nip out
41	*Hugh*	You don't think it's a natural tree?
42	*James*	No
43	*Hugh*	Do you think he's talking about his feelings?
44	*James*	Or just his hatred of his friend
45	*Shan*	What does foe mean?
46	*James*	Enemy
47	*Hugh*	I think he was angry first of all
48	*Shan*	What does wiles mean? Like someone's wily?
49	*Hugh*	OK let's go through. What do you think of the first verse? He was angry with someone and he tried to keep his anger sort of trapped down.

		Well, that's it. What about the second one?
50	*Marion*	It kept growing and growing and he didn't say anything
51	*James*	He was angry with his foe
52	*Hugh*	What does the next verse mean?
53	*James*	No his hate grew in him, because he was scared of his foe
54	*Hugh*	He tried to cover up and smile over his fears
55	*Shan*	And his anger grew both day and night
56	*Joan*	Yes
57	*Shan*	Where's the apple?
58	*Marion*	On the tree
59	*James*	It's not a real tree!
60	*Shan*	No it isn't, it's his anger
61	*Hugh*	It's his anger growing like a tree
62	*Shan*	Maybe he took his anger out on somebody and killed them

The teacher commented on this as follows:

The great significance of transcriptions for the teacher is that it allows some insight into learning as a process, and for the child that the importance of talk is reinforced, and that the child sees objectively the value of his or her words. . . . Unaided small-group discussion is a preliminary to whole group discussion.

I've omitted so far one of the most interesting little exchanges on the transcript. After Shan's question at 28 (And did someone steal the apple from the tree?) this happens:

29		(yes/no)
30	*Kate*	Like Snow White
31	*Hugh*	Yes, someone did try to steal it . . .

Kate's analogy is interesting not just because it shows clearly a common process, of recognizing connections between the new thing and what is already known, in an attempt to find the familiar in the unknown, but because she has picked up the feeling tone at the centre of the poem without knowing it. The analogy with Snow White is in some ways accurate, because the world of Snow White and fairy tale, with its powerful, archetypal images and symbols (see Friedlander 1947, Bettelheim 1977) has the same resonance that Blake's poem has here. Apples, trees of life and death, are reminders of the world of myth and fairy tale.

We see from this transcript that a group of fourteen-year-olds can, unaided, get close enough to the central meaning of a complex poem to discover a satisfactory interpretation: they do it in their own way, with no promptings from the teacher, no barrage of questions which the teacher will signify they have answered correctly or wrongly, and no anxieties or tensions. The implications of this experience could be enormous: they may learn from it, if the teacher's response is sensitive enough, that they *can* do these things, that they can tackle and solve difficult problems together in talk, and that each of them can share and participate in the process, as all six of the students do here.

In case these conclusions seem too grandiose, here is an even briefer extract from the transcript of another group in the same class:

Steve	'And in the morning glad I see My foe outstretched beneath the tree' The relief there when he sees his foe. I mean all that trouble he's been going through with that apple – and deceiving his foe
Ann	I think he's killed him myself –
Carol	What – destroyed his –
Ann	Killed his foe
Steve	Well in his mind or actually?
Ann	Actually
Steve	With all these things he's supposed to have bottled up
Carol	He's destroyed the element that's causing –
Ann	The apple right, is all his fears that've come out eventually
Carol } *Steve* }	Yeah

*   *   *   *

Ann	He's physically killed him. But that's it in a metaphor sort of way
Steve	I suppose so
Carol	Yes because the foe is the element – the reason for all these fears – and so he's destroyed it to rid himself of that . . .

In that moment of talk, the same investment by individuals and the same collaborative building of meaning by the group are in evidence, but heightened by a social cohesiveness which facilitates the expression of thoughts and feelings.

Here, because the subject is a poem and concerns emotions, the students talk to explore their emotional and intellectual responses. But sometimes it is not so much 'response' that is at issue but 'understanding'. Although we have argued earlier that the two are not as separable as is often assumed, quite clearly the balance between them will be different if the topic is, say, a physical phenomenon rather than an emotionally charged piece of language. We would expect the talk of students encountering the concept of gravity to be rather different. Here is an example of such talk with another dimension of difference added by the age of the two participants, eight-year-old boys.

Gravity

Carl and Michael are eight. Carl already knows something about gravity and has been trying to help Michael understand it. 'It's a sort of pressure that keeps us on the earth,' he says; 'it's surrounding us now. If we just walk, we're walking through gravity. . . . If you've ever thrown a ball into the air, it always comes down again. That's because gravity pushes it down.' For Michael, it's a new concept. He has to identify what it refers to, or perhaps try to abstract a common feature from the cases Carl mentions – people being kept on the earth, a ball falling down. He has already tried to relate it to himself in the only way he can.

Michael	So if you was trying to ride up a hill with your bike. On my bike it's very difficult
Carl	Well that's because the gravity's trying to push you down
Michael	Oh so that's why you go so fast down hills? . . . the gravity won't push you up?

Now he tries to fit it into his whole scheme of things, but it keeps going wrong.

Michael	You know Carl scientists believe that a volcano blew up and that could have been made out of a volcano, 'cos lava didn't come out of that volcano
Carl	Well, lava –

Michael	Gravity – that stuff what you just said – that came out of it, that's what scientists believe
Carl	What came out? Gravity? No, gravity doesn't come out of the volcano
Michael	No but it's a very special volcano
Carl	Yes, well there's never been a very special volcano. Just lava
Michael	I know, but lava might have dried up into gravity
Carl	No, because the gravity isn't all dry 'cos it's –
Michael	Unless it must have – it might have been the water
Carl	Well, if it would have been the water it would – we would bob up. It would make us go up and down
Michael	Ah, unless it would be sort of smoke
Carl	No, it can't be sort of smoke. If it's smoke all the world would be black and you'd only see a little bit through it
Michael	Yeah
Carl	Really, it's sort of invisible, it's invisible
Michael	So we're – so we're – so we're covered with gravity now?
Carl	Yes. It's under our feet, and over our feet really. It's trying to push down skyscrapers and things like that but because they've got the cement there to help them, they don't fall. Right?

Michael is clearly trying to evolve some kind of image of what gravity might be. Carl sees it already as a force, and although he is hazy about details has a notion of it as a *process* rather than a *thing*. But Michael can only begin to make sense of it by trying on different ways of seeing it, none of which exactly fit, because there's nothing in his experience quite like it. He draws on knowledge he already has: what naturally-created stuff does he know that would have the effects of this stuff Carl is describing? Lava? Water? Smoke? He tests each one, and each one Carl rejects, by using his own familiar understandings. There were never 'special volcanoes'; water supports, it doesn't 'push down'; smoke would have its own effects. Michael ends up with no clear ideas of what gravity is – but some glimmering of what it isn't.

Something else is worth noting: that the boys tackle this knowledge without a teacher there to help them and that the teacher has trusted them enough to be certain that they will do it and will learn. The process is conducted entirely in their language and with their habitual sorts of strategies, their ways of going at a problem. Our adult language works very differently from theirs, and could have got in the way. Adults who know tend to present their knowledge 'by the book' – with a linear, sequential, logical organization. Learners have to make different sorts of patterns – 'holding patterns' in the first place, ones that connect the new idea to what is already known. They need to use bits of knowledge from wherever they can find them to illuminate the new idea – not only from previous lessons in the subject but from out-of-school experience, books read, TV programmes and films, conversations – in fact from the whole process of having been alive up to this moment. This is what the Bullock Report is talking about when it says: 'In order to accept what is offered when we are told something, we have to have somewhere to put it; and having somewhere to put it means that the framework of past knowledge and experience into which it must fit is adequate as a means of interpreting and apprehending it' (4.9).

It is striking that these two boys sustain this difficult talk without the teacher being there. It is, of course, largely because of her that they do it: she encouraged them to talk about gravity, they know she will be interested to hear what they say, and the tape-recorder, in a sense, represents her. But many teachers would be worried that she is not there to correct Michael's misunderstandings. Carl, it is true, can tell him he is wrong, but does not know enough to give Michael the understanding he needs.

This is an issue of some importance. The thesis of this chapter, and, indeed, this book, is that students have to construct their own understanding; but if the understanding that is constructed is false, the value of the process is hard to see. Michael certainly committed himself to a series of false propositions about gravity. But this is, in fact, in the nature of 'coming to know', and is probably both inevitable and necessary. Where the phenomena concerned are ones which, like bikes going faster downhill, are familiar to us, we tend to start out not from a blank absence of explanatory ideas but from fairly definite conceptions which happen to be erroneous. When someone talks about what sounds to us like a new kind of 'stuff', what can we do in the first place – especially if we are eight – but relate it to whatever other strange stuffs we have previously come across, like lava? We start from error, not from nothing, and the process is bound to be one of successive approximation to the truth, or of searching for relevant analogies. For Michael to move into an active consideration of alternative possibilities represents a step forward in his development of an adequate concept. And it is difficult to imagine that an adult definition, supplied by the teacher, would have been of any help.

Nevertheless, one might still ask whether a teacher who was helping them in more subtle ways might have enabled them to get further. Perhaps; but not necessarily. The next example faces us squarely with the effects of 'teaching' upon learners.

Molecular theory

A first-year mixed-ability class in a comprehensive school have been doing a circus of experiments on molecular theory: that is to say, there are some fourteen experiments set up round the lab, and the class, in small groups of three to four, move round them. The idea is that each experiment, in a different way, will confirm and illustrate the basic theory of molecules that the science department wants them to understand at this stage.

Three boys have been performing one particular experiment: a wire is suspended between two points, and a weight is hung on the wire. When an electric current is run through the wire so that it becomes red hot, the weight is seen to be lowered – it

1	*Teacher*	What's happened then lads?
2	*Boy A*	That went down
3	*Teacher*	Why?
4	*Boys*	Because it's a weight.
		It's heating up
		Because of the molecules

'goes down', in the boys' words. While they were watching the experiment, they had a serious disagreement about whether the wire was 'stretching' or not: two boys said it was, the third said it wasn't. It isn't ignorance that leads us to fail to understand a new term if in our experience it already carries a quite satisfactory meaning. What does 'expansion' mean? There are special problems when the everyday meaning of a term overlaps but is not quite fully matched with the sense it has in a specialized field. A teacher may feel the term has been explained satisfactorily, and the things he or she hears and reads may confirm that. But the surface may belie the depths. It seemed as though there was some confusion about whether 'stretched' things return to their original size or not: One boy said:

It doesn't stretch, or it wouldn't go up any more

and later

It stretches, but it doesn't make it go any longer or looser

At the point where the argument is getting acrimonious, the science teacher arrives. With the advantage of hindsight and the calmness of not being in the hurly-burly of the laboratory, let's see what happens, and to what extent the boys learn anything, and the teacher teaches anything.

There was no way he could have known it, but this was the wrong question, because it doesn't show him what the boys have been talking about, and so he doesn't learn about their confusion. He ought perhaps to have asked 'What have you been saying about what you saw?'

What kind of answer did he expect or hope for? It looks from what happens as though he hoped to hear something approximating to the 'correct' scientific explanation. See 12 and 27 below.

He gets three simultaneous answers, and either because of a deliberate choice, or because he hears only the 'right' answer, he selects the answer that matches in with the basic concept. The other two, correct but not really 'right', he disregards.

5	*Teacher*	What's heating it up?
6	*Boys B & C*	The molecules
7	*Boy A*	Electricity
8	*Teacher*	Electricity's heating it up, yes, that's making it hot, when it gets hot what's happening to the molecules in it?
9	*Boy C*	They're moving around, pushing up and down
10	*Teacher*	They're moving around because they've got – ?
11	*Boy C*	They've got electricity in them energy
12	*Teacher*	Energy, that's right, they've got energy so they move around more. Like you, if you've got lots of energy, you move around don't you? OK, so they've got lots of energy, they move up and down, they move round about, they move a lot more. What do they need if they move around more?
13	*Boy C*	They need er – more electricity, sir
14	*Teacher*	Eh?
15	*Boy C*	They need more electricity
16	*Teacher*	To make them move around more, yes, if they're moving around a lot more, what happens to them then? What do they do to the wire?

Again he has a choice, and again he chooses only the 'correct' answer. But now he too uses the term the boys have been struggling to use – molecules. It might be clear already that two of the boys at least are not too sure about it.

He accepts the formulation in the boy's own words – moving around – but then uses one of the most common strategies any teacher can use: the statement left uncompleted, which acts as a test question: 'read my mind and tell me what word I think should go in that space'. Well, is it electricity or energy? Exactly what does this lad think is happening inside the wire?
He attempts to bring the whole thing within the experience of the boys, by his analogy with their having 'lots of energy'. Whether the meaning of energy in its everyday sense is the same as its meaning in physics is something that is glossed over for the moment. Then onto another question; for the teacher, the answer is presumably obvious, because the train of thought he's following is clear to him; but to the boys it's yet another closed question – there's clearly a 'right' answer, but they don't know what it might be.

Well, that's a safe bet. If they needed electricity to give them energy in the first place, then as they move around more, they presumably need more energy, so – more electricity?
How will the teacher deal with this? Will he recognize that the question he asked wasn't the right one, and how will he signal the kind of direction he wants?
He accepts what the boy said, and pivots nicely to lead into a different way of getting at what he wants – 'What do they do to the wire?' But there is still the problem of the gap between what he knows about what is happening, and the sense the boys can make of it.

17 *Boy C*   They – they stretch it as *it's coming up (?)*

18 *Teacher*   *Yes they need* more room. If you move around a lot you need more room, so they need more room so they make the wire – ?

19 *Boy C*   Longer

20 *Teacher*   Longer? Do they make it thicker as well do you think? Or not?

21 *Boy B*   No

22 *Boy C*   They make it thinner

Again that word 'stretch'! And we see here the real problem with the word: as the talk continues (17–25): the boys are using the everyday meaning of the word, which is not the same as the concept of 'expansion'.

The teacher talks over the second half of what the boy says: he hears the first part, with the word 'stretch', and his response inevitably reformulates that into something which more closely approximates to the way he wants it to be. And again, he leaves the boys to say one word to complete an utterance.

Given the interpretations the boys have made, this is inevitable, and in its own way at least partially correct. But to the teacher it's less than half of the story, because 'expansion' is so much more than 'stretching'.

This kind of question is usually a signal to pupils that there was something wrong with the first answer: few teachers who conduct this kind of question and answer dialogue will ever say 'No, that's wrong'. Instead, they signal in various ways that the answer was unsatisfactory. The 'Or not?' is an attempt to make it a genuine choice: the teacher is presumably conscious that what he is doing is foreclosing on possibilities for the pupils, and so adds the tag to make it less of a closed question. It doesn't, of course, work.

Since utterance 7, only Boy C has said anything. Why that was, one can't say; and what the other two boys were thinking during their prolonged silence, one can't say either. But Boy B was the one who was adamant that the wire wasn't 'stretching'; and yet he too is, like the other lad, not yet able to see what the teacher is getting at. This may be, in fact, not because of any understanding or lack of it, but because of the increasingly narrowing effect of this kind of questioning. What seems to happen is that the point of the dialogue becomes purely the answering of the most recent question in a way that will satisfy the teacher; when only one person is controlling the direction the dialogue is taking, and the other people are basically passive, then the students tend to lose faith in their own knowledge, or to feel that what they know is less important than what they say at this precise minute. Satisfying the teacher becomes more important than satisfying oneself intellectually.

23 *Teacher*   They make it thinner do they? If you want more room, do you just go in one direction and then shorten the room in the other direction, do you think, or –

24 *Boy C*   No (laughs)

25 *Teacher*   If you wanted more room, you'd make the room bigger in both directions, wouldn't you? So do you think they might want to make it thicker as well?

26 *Boy C*   Yes they might make it thicker.

27 *Teacher*   Yes, so there's more energy, they're moving around more, it gets longer and it gets –

28 *Boys A & C*   Thicker

29 *Teacher*   But the weight in this case might make it a little bit thinner. But er – not really. It should be making it thicker. If it gets hotter it gets thicker as well as

He still hasn't had the answer he wants. What else could he have done? Well, he could have stopped that particular line of dialogue, and said 'The wire expands. What does expansion mean to you?' The answer would have shown him precisely where the pupils were in their understanding of this fundamental concept; and perhaps he'd have been able to do something about it. But perhaps that would have been too frightening; this experiment, for these three boys, was the twelfth of fourteen experiments: if they still didn't understand basic concepts at this stage, a teacher might well feel something was wrong. So it is, of course.

Does he laugh because he's recognized the implications of his narrow definition? Or because he feels that the teacher has made something like a joke and he ought to laugh at it? Or because he's feeling uncertain and uncomfortable at the whole situation? Or . . . ?

What is the 'they' supposed to refer to? Presumably it's the molecules. Is it then the molecules that make the wire thicker or thinner? Where does that leave the energy mentioned previously? And just what is it that happens inside this wire – if it is 'inside' the wire?

When pupils make the right response, teachers tend to assume that they have understood it. If the *teacher* said that, it would be embedded in the whole network of knowledge and assumptions that is 'physics'; so, now that the boys have said the right thing, everyone's happy, because they've understood it. Except that they probably haven't; they've said it because the inexorable logic of this kind of dialogue means that they have to say it to get off the hook. The tentativeness of Boy C's 'might' shows he's still not too clear about it all.

Presumably the teacher now feels he's summarizing what's been said: in fact he's reformulating, particularly what he himself has said. Yet again he leaves the boys to add one word to complete an utterance.

Which they dutifully do. And the third boy now says something, too.

Thoughtfully, he tries to make them feel that what they said about it getting thinner wasn't completely wrong; but what the effect of this afterthought is on their concept of 'expansion' isn't at all clear.

longer. OK? Right you're going to
draw it and write it up now?

And at this point, the teacher moves off to the next group of
children who are calling for his attention. At the time, he felt
only that he'd satisfactorily helped one group of boys to understand what they were doing. It was afterwards, when he saw the
tape and transcript that had been made and looked at it closely
that he felt depressed as he recognized the abyss between what
he'd hoped was happening and what actually happened.

If we ask what the boys were learning, the answer seems to be
that it is more to do with how to cope in science lessons than
with understanding molecular theory. They are using their
language not to think about science but to defend themselves
and to satisfy their teacher. The teacher himself, despite all his
skill and his understanding of the physics, finds himself unable
to help the students to a similar understanding. To see why this
might be, we need to reaffirm an important notion.

III
Students have to conduct their thinking in their own language.
The intimacy and private nature of thinking demand that. But
their language is not static. Under the demands of the functions
it has to perform, and influenced by the language the learner
meets, it develops. One way it develops is by incorporating the
terminology of the disciplines, building it in as additional resources for thinking. This important part of school learning is
a matter of simultaneously acquiring new words and discovering
new things, as we saw with the students who were grappling with
'chaetae' and 'gravity'. Doughty et al. (1972) outlined the stages
a learner seems to go through in acquiring new terms:

Stage 1 Familiarizations
It is very often a stage of silence and apparent passivity. It may
look like apathy or an apparent unwillingness to participate in
discussion because it is silent. It's most obvious the first term

And what is it they'll write up? As the dialogue has gone on, he's moved them steadily towards the kind of formulation of the theories that he previously gave them himself. But looking at what they say themselves, it seems clear enough that they have little comprehension of what has happened: in important ways, they haven't even been able to agree on whether they all saw the same thing happen, let alone why.

---

after starting an O-level or CSE course, or beginning a sixth-form course.

Stage 2 Rehearsal
Individual items – words, names, etc. – are likely to be used hesitantly, with an intonation that shows the speaker is uncertain about the terms. During this stage, learners can be so preoccupied with their own difficulties in understanding that they may find it hard to listen and attend to what others are saying.

Stage 3 Trial performance
Still hesitant and tentative, but the intonation will not show uncertainty. Learners recognize the term when others use it, and can appreciate its implications.

Stage 4 Fluent use
The students use the terms with their full meanings, naturally and easily. The words have become part of their normal vocabulary, and are readily available to the students, who are able to handle confidently the concepts they refer to.

Some sixth formers, reminiscing at the end of their biology course about what they had to do, recall that it was difficult to learn about enzymes.

Teacher Why were they difficult?
Pupil 1 There were so many, and they all sounded the same
Teacher Were you learning parrot-fashion, to remember them, or learning what the enzymes were?
Pupil 1 Learning what they *did*
Teacher What do you remember feeling the first time you came across a word like peristalsis?
Pupil 2 Here we go again, another long word (laughter)

Pupil 3   We didn't really know what it was until we'd heard it several times

These students were successful: but a teacher, looking back in writing at her experience of science at school, defines what happens when learners are expected to be confident 'fluent users' without being allowed and encouraged to move through the other stages.

When I think of the science I did at school, it's no wonder I hated it. All the long words that we were expected to know and all the technical details that seemed so important – more important, it seems, than my enjoyment of what I was doing.

What is needed when new terms and concepts come up is not primarily elaboration by the teacher but elaboration by the pupils with the teacher paying attention to what they say, as in the example that follows. After an exchange like this the teacher is in a better position to help because it will be clearer what they do or do not understand. This teacher has asked, 'What's an atom?'

Pupil 1   What's an atom? I don't know
Pupil 2   It's a – er – particle
Pupils   A particle
Pupil 1   Yes, everything's made out of them – that is, and that is, and that is, and that is, and everything is (pointing to various things)
Pupil 3   This table is
Pupil 4   This table's made up out of atoms and that
Pupil 5   Everything's made up out of particles – particles of atoms and molecules
Teacher   Well, why is that book different from the table then?
Pupil 1   It's not
Pupil 4   Because it's solid
Pupil 1   It's not, it's made of nearly the same thing, isn't it – molecules
Pupil 6   Paper used to be wood really, used to be the same thing, but it was (?) and changed

Pupil 6 raises a point that occurs to him as being relevant:

tables and paper are both made from wood. In fact, this is a different issue from the fact that both are composed of atoms and molecules, but it takes some thinking to recognize that it *is* different; and this thinking, though apparently tangential to the matter in hand, is part of learning about atoms. The relationship between associated pieces of knowledge needs to be explored for any one of them to be securely 'acquired'.

This kind of early mulling over and rehearsal of terms and ideas is crucial. If it doesn't happen, then the pupils can remain with unresolved confusions, without even knowing they are confused. It happens in talk all the time, especially small-group talk without a teacher: but it can and should happen in writing too. If the writer is relaxed and feels secure enough to think aloud on to paper, then the learning power of that kind of writing is very marked; the permanence of writing means that the writer can inspect his or her own ideas more carefully, both in the act of writing and afterwards too. Equally, if the writer can choose the form and the language in which to operate, then it is more likely that the writing will mirror the movement of thought, and that we should be able to gain insights into the learner's understanding from the writing, just as we can from talk.

Writing works in that way in the following case, where we see learners coping with the tension between having to accept someone else's language, and having, or being able, to work on one's own. Here, first, is a textbook definition of 'solubility', the kind of definition that can be learnt off and produced when requested:

> A solution is a homogeneous mixture of two or more substances. As matter is now [the textbook is dated 1970] regarded as discontinuous (molecular), complete homogeneity is impossible, but for true solution we must imagine the particles to be of molecular dimensions and to be uniformly distributed.

A student may well be expected to have a grasp of that; but compare it with this:

> A named substance which will dissolve into water. That the water takes the substance, staturates [sic] it, and breaks it down into small molecules eventually dissolving the substances into the water.

Thus a second-year sixth student, aged seventeen, invited to write down a definition of 'solubility' entirely in her own words at the beginning of a session. She then had seven unnamed substances to put into liquids, to stir, and then to heat: she had to note what happened when the substance was put into the liquid, when the test tube was boiled and finally after one and a half hours to write a second definition of 'solubility'. To repeat, attentive reading of pupils' writing should give us some clues to their understanding of what's going on.

Substance
A Quickly dissolved into water
B Took a long time to dissolve
C Crackles, but did not completely dissolve
D
E Took a long time to get the residue
F Partically (sic) set on the surface of the water
G Took quite a long time to dissolve but eventually took in a considerable number of crystals

Heating
A Water after being boiled appeared to be clearer.
B It boiled, residue bubbled at the base but nothing important happened.
C Residue appeared to be a solid mass which when water boiled it appeared to mix into the water and as soon as it was below boiling point it regained its previous solid state. On heating, mixture bumped up and down as water began to boil.
D Boils and dissolves residue.
E Doubles the amount of liquid in tube. Residue at base boiled.
F Boiled and went solid.
G Went much clearer when heated.

Solubility
It is very difficult to define solubility accurately as many factors have to be taken into consideration. The most important I would consider to be the solvent and the temperature that the solvent is when the substance is added. Also what happens to the substances and the solvent when the temperature is taken above or below its original level.

I would suppose that a substance is considered soluble when once it is dissolved into the liquid no degree of temperature will separate it from the liquid.

The student was a non-scientist doing a science course, which accounts for the 'unscientific language', but her increased grasp of the issues, and the growth of tentativeness is striking. Her fellow students equally found a change in their original concepts, and their writing too shows the reader something of what is going on:

1   When a substance is cooled its powers of absorbing and dissolving substances are low.

2   Solubility is when any form of substance can be dissolved in a liquid until the point comes when the liquid cannot dissolve any more, but if the liquid is heated thus using up the space more of the substance can be dissolved, as the space between the molecules of liquid become bigger.

3   Substances vary in the degree to which they will dissolve in a liquid. There are many factors that will influence the amount of substance that will dissolve: (a) volume of liquid (b) type of liquid (c) temperature of liquid (d) size of molecules and particles of substance. When a substance has been dissolved in a volume of water (or any other liquid) – *solvent* – so that no more will dissolve and a residue is left then we say the solution is saturated. However if we heat this solution we will find that the residue dissolves and according to the type of solute being used, even more of it will be dissolved in the hot solution.

One consequence of this work was that the students were more sensitive to possibilities than they had been, but there were other more general effects, too: they were able to go back to the original textbook and ask their own questions about its limitations, and they became less likely to use terms like 'water', 'soluble' and 'dissolve' in the indefinite ways they had done. But in addition they had discovered for themselves how writing makes things permanent so that the writer can return to them;

how re-reading their own early definitions made them reflect on what they had previously thought, and on how their opinions had changed; and how the recording of the observations, in the language they had available, both drew their attention to what they were looking at, and made them aware of the strengths and gaps in their language. They became aware of what they could and could not say easily: the struggle to express new thoughts put them at the frontier of both their own language, and of learning itself.

When students make their provisional interpretations of facts and ideas, they need to use their own language, because it is readily available, adaptable, and something they feel comfortable with. As this language expands, by incorporating new terms, it becomes more able to cope with academic learning, as the last section described. But development in language is not marked only by new vocabulary: there are other ways in which it moves closer to the language in which expert adults handle knowledge. New structures are developed, new strategies for presenting ideas are devised, and new sorts of communicative purposes are internalized. At least, this is what the encounter with the adult language of the disciplines, particularly through books, ought to lead to. Unfortunately, the effect is often very different, and the result can be that instead of offering access to new resources, books can block the way. We must ask why this should be so, before looking briefly at the process of learning to use book-language as it should be.

IV

It may seem strange that we have been speaking of different languages, the language of the pupil and the language of the teacher and of the textbook writer, when all three parties use English. And indeed, the differences between them are not analogous to those between English and French, where the gap is bridged by translation – the substitution of words and phrases in one language for words and phrases in another. The differences here are not of a kind that can be solved by translation into 'simple language', because they are too profound. The distance between the two may often be such that the writing of a student who is attempting to acquire the new language can read almost like that of a foreigner who is not at ease with English:

Measuring the surface area of animals
Place your specimen (the most suitable of which being a

small rodent) onto a piece of paper, not required for further use after the experiments completion, but still sufficiently clean as to cause no arm to the mammal. Mark with a single straight line the point at which the animal's body tapers away to form the animal's tail. After removing from the paper your specimen cut along this line, and disregard as waste the piece which has been cut away. Return to the paper your animal, and carefully bend the paper till it completely encircles the mammal, also record in some way the length of paper necessary in order to completely encircle a single time the mammal. Cut away the remaining paper, and you will find yourself left with a piece of paper roughly equal to the total surface area of your original mammal.

By now weighing the animal, and dividing the animal's weight into it surface area, results of use in later experiments may be obtained.

The apparent inability of students to understand the language of textbooks is one of the difficulties teachers most often complain of. For instance a worksheet question asks: 'In which areas were the Apaches most active?' There is a strange verb form in Jan's answer:

In California, where a succession of fine priests worked, did Spain succeed in her colonial dreams . . .

When we try to account for it, we find the reason by looking at the book she was 'working from', in which this construction was used:

Only in California, where a succession of fine priests worked, did Spain succeed in her colonial dreams . . .

The difficulties in understanding what she was reading and doing were evidently great enough for her to abandon any idea of answering the question. Instead, she tries to cope with it by copying: and demonstrates, as verbatim but incorrect copying of this kind generally does, that she doesn't understand what she is writing about. But the fault is only partly in her 'ability': it is also in the nature of the language she is expected to cope with.

Such unfamiliar forms are common in school books, where they are less likely to be pinpointed by teachers as possible sources of trouble than are difficult words. 'A man walks four miles in 55 minutes.' Which man? Where? Why? Isn't some phrase like 'every day' missing from the end, accounting for that 'walks' rather than 'walked'? 'Let x be 4.' Who's stopping it? Constructions are used quite freely which simply don't occur in the everyday language of most students.

But what above all makes book language alien is neither its vocabulary nor its constructions but the whole nature of its assumptions. Such books look as though they are meant to inform; but not only do most students not say things in these ways, they do not say them for those reasons. In itself, of course, giving information is a familiar everyday function, but it is usually carried out with a clear immediate purpose: explicitly or implicitly, part of the message is 'This will amuse you', or 'This shows you're wrong' or 'You'd better know this because of what you're likely to do.' But no such specific and comprehensible reasons appear to lie behind the information that textbook writers give. Students who seek in the text for some clue as to what it all means to the writer, and is supposed to mean to them, are disappointed. The information is simply given, as in log tables, without the slightest interest being expressed in how it will be received and used. In fact, however, the communicative purpose behind the writing may be a real one: the writer may intend to make the truth available to whoever might need it, and for whatever purpose. But such a generalized concern is remote from the intentions that inform our everyday exchanges, and it is one that students only slowly come to find intelligible, and rarely when they are still at school. The growth of that sort of purpose in themselves is an important aspect of moving into a fully adult role, but until they have begun to experience it, they will inevitably fail to detect the human voice behind the language of informative books. In the same way, students still ask 'What do I have to do?' even though they have read the 'clear, simple instructions' on the worksheet: they have failed to see that the author is actually speaking to them, explaining to them what they have to do.

Sometimes, of course, textbook language really is as devoid of a felt communicative purpose as it seems to the student, perhaps because it was made by boiling down other books rather than being the product of an original mind actively engaged with a topic. But behind good 'transactional' language there does lie a person's warm intent. The concern of the scientist or historian to clear up confusion and set the record straight may be as personal and as intense a drive as the one that leads to the more openly displayed emotion of poetry; but it will fail to communicate itself to the inexperienced reader because it finds expression not in emotive language, but in the very energy and force of the argument itself.

> This collective self-consciousness was indeed the great spiritual gain of the Industrial Revolution, against which the disruption of an older and in many ways more humanly comprehensible way of life must be set. It was perhaps a unique formation, this British working class of 1832. The slow, piecemeal accretions of capital accumulation had meant that the preliminaries to the Industrial Revolution stretched back for hundreds of years. From Tudor times onwards this artisan culture had grown more complex with each phase of technical and social change. Delaney, Dekker and Nashe: Winstanley and Lilburne: Bunyan and Defoe – all had at times addressed themselves to it. Enriched by the experiences of the seventeenth century, carrying through the eighteenth century the intellectual and libertarian traditions which we have described, forming their own traditions of mutuality in the friendly society and trades club, these men did not pass, in one generation, from the peasantry to the new industrial town. They suffered the experience of the Industrial Revolution as articulate, free-born Englishmen. Those who were sent to gaol might know the Bible better than those on the Bench, and those who were transported to Van Diemen's Land might ask their relatives to send Cobbett's *Register* after them.

> (E. P. Thompson *The Making of the English Working Class* Penguin edition, p. 913)

The sustained enumeration of the achievements of the centuries, the juxtaposition of the most inclusive generalities with pithy detail, the panache of the naming, the confidence of the rhythms, all display the conviction and commitment of the writer.

How can students move towards language like this? How can exposure to well written arguments lead to a growth in their own competence rather than a sense of confrontation with a cold and alien style? Only, we suggest, by experiencing for themselves something of Thompson's purpose: that is, by finding themselves in the position of having something worth while to say, a contribution to make, if not to the world at least to their peers or their teacher. The element in Thompson's achievement which we must hold on to is the sense of this writer urgently desiring that his readers see what is so clear to him. *This* is the pattern in it all, he is saying.

When young writers are trying to do the same sort of thing that Thompson is trying to do, the features of his writing style will be seen as enabling resources that they can tentatively apply themselves. Compositions that read simply like imitations and exercises, on the other hand, come from mimicking of the surface features of adult discourse, without any recognition of the purposes that lie behind those features. Young writers must be asked in the end, after considering everything, to write only what they see. Their writings must be authentic communications of things they feel to be worth communicating, written out of a desire to share. What needs fostering is not certain forms of language, but intellectual curiosity, autonomy of judgment and a climate in which individual viewpoints are encouraged and taken seriously. Out of that commitment grows the kind of language use that all teachers want to see.

The piece of writing that follows shows this commitment: there is a sense of a shrewd mind with something to say and a concern for the reader. But then the readers are a small group that the writer has been working with for several weeks, each individual on a separate but related topic, and in this writing he is genuinely telling them what he has found out, and he anticipates that they will want to know. He is fourteen.

The '49 Gold Rush

The first people started to enter California around 1790 and by 1846 people were beginning to settle. On the 24/1/1848 a man called James Marshall was investigating a ditch in California when he found GOLD and this of course is where the gold rush began. For people living on the east side of America in towns like New York, Philadelphia and Boston there was two routes to the west, one was by clipper around Cape Horn which took 130 days or by covered Wagon which ment you would have to go over three hard hurdles

(i) the Rocky Mountains, (ii) the Great Basin (Desert) and (iii) the Sierra Nevada mountains. The people who went by covered Wagon often took *all* there belongings which of course slowed the mules down very much. I suppose most of the people got over the Rockys but when they got to the Great Basin many lost there lives, in fact in 1849 (peak of the gold rush) 50,000 men, women and children lost their lives. The Sierra Nevada was proberly the hardest of the three mainly because they were very tired and that the Sierra Nevada was very steep. It was so steep at the last two miles that it took 10 mules to pull and ten men to push, but sometimes they linked the wagons going down with the ones coming up to help them, and other times all the mules were put together to take one wagon up at a time. The Clippers which was the other way round to California was realy just an easy way of making money for the captains and a rase to see who could do it in the fastest time. The ship was paid for with only one journey to California and the ship that held the record for the fastest time was called the *Flying Cloud* and he did the journey in half the normal time.

This language is not the written-down speech of the student: it shows the influence of books. Not so much in its vocabulary, but in its systematic laying out of the information. For all its expressive features – 'GOLD', '*all*', 'really just an easy way' – it reads like written language and it works as a piece of informing. What the young writer has taken from books is not stylistic features, nor superficial imitation, but a way of going about the job of explaining; and the reason he is able to apply what he has learnt is that explaining is what he is really doing. If he continues to have the opportunity to pursue real purposes in this way, more and more of the strategies of mature written discourse will present themselves to him as functional and efficient means of achieving those purposes.

So far we have suggested that 'learning' isn't the name of a distinctive mental event, but is those varied processes that result in a change in a person's consciousness. We have identified some of these processes and have grouped them under three general headings: 'handling the elements', 'handling the generalizations and ideas', and 'finding personal significance'. The processes could be characterized in other ways: the essential point is that they involve working on the knowledge in a vigorous and personal way. Our next major point was that although these are essentially mental operations, they are intimately linked to language, often occur overtly in speech and writing and could with great benefit be induced to take those forms more generally. Since this means encouraging children to express themselves in their own language, the implication is that we must accept their inevitable forms of expression and work with them. But although when we first look at it, we can feel that children's language is defective and deficient, we soon perceive it differently: partly this is because we begin to read it sympathetically, and listen with attention; but also, the language itself develops. The very attention we are now paying to it and the planned introduction of the special vocabulary of the disciplines, together with the exposure to good examples of the written language, help in this. But above all, their language inevitably develops because the learners are using it as the principal means of learning.

Contexts for language

It is time to see what teachers and students achieve together when the kinds of ideas we have been discussing are put into practice. Successful practice will justify change, and that is what we hope to illustrate in the next two chapters with a series of case studies. There are constant themes in all of them, first mentioned in the chapter 'Generalizations', pp. 14–16. The learners are at the centre of the experience; their previous knowledge is deliberately activated and brought into contact with the new material; they are encouraged to use their own immediate and personal language resources; and the teachers see their job as being to present the students with activities which will simultaneously interest them enough to make them want to pursue them, and make available to them an understanding of the processes of learning through language.

I

A teacher of nine-year-olds had obtained a bull's eye from a friend who was a biology teacher in a secondary school. Following the directions the biologist had given her, she dissected it in front of those of her class who were interested in watching. She talked them through it, and they commented on it as she went. A day or so later, she offered as a possible assignment a card of questions, plus a labelled diagram of the eye. Anyone who wanted to could take the card and answer the questions by talking with a tape-recorder. Two girls, Sharon and Nicola, took up the option and went off with the questions and a tape-recorder.

1 Describe how to dissect an eye and what it looks like inside.
2 Why do we need eyes?
3 Why don't plants need eyes?
4 Some animals have eyes in the front of their heads, and some at the sides. Think of a cow, a monkey and a lion. Why are their eyes different?

5   What is the blind spot? How can you find it?

6   Where does the optic nerve go?

7   When you read, how much does your eye help you to understand words? How much does your brain?

8   Talk about anything else about the eye that interests you.

The girls spent over 30 minutes on their own, recording and talking about the questions: the transcript runs to seven closely typed pages.

Conventionally, when teachers ask questions on worksheets, they expect written answers. If we ask why, the answers all have to do with things that are to the teacher's advantage: it's easier to mark; you can't mark and assess talk, but you can writing; you can see immediately if the pupils have understood; you can tell who's working; and so on. But nothing much happens at the other end, unless the questions are of the kind that can *only be answered in writing*. As Nancy Martin *et al.* (1977) points out in relation to a particular worksheet her team looked at, the best type of question was:

> the imaginative one which has allowed the student to deal with feelings as well as facts. Perhaps it is the only one of the three 'answers' which needs to be written down rather than said. If the other two questions had been answered orally perhaps a discussion would have developed which would have been more useful, or, at any rate, more interesting than Adam's single sentence.

Questions for learning should be ones that you want to answer, and the answer should be in a form that's appropriate to that kind of question. So the first point here is that these questions are designed to be talked about. Writing, if it occurs, will have a different genesis, and be serving different purposes altogether.

The questions about the eye are tapping different kinds of latent interests in the children; but they also signal different possibilities in the original experience. None of them is meant for the teacher to check on how right the pupils have got it: ideas like 'literal comprehension', in which a judge will assess how much readers have understood, are teaching-focussed rather than learning-focussed. These questions help the girls to unpick their experience and to give it several different kinds of meaning. There are questions (1 and 8) that encourage them to talk over what they actually saw and felt. There are two questions (5 and 6) that you might call 'anatomical'. There are three questions (2, 3 and 4) which are teleological and direct the girls' attention to notions they may never have thought of before. And question 7 arises from a particular interest of the teacher's, and her intention to introduce her pupils to a more sophisticated idea of the basic language process of reading than they might otherwise have had.

That they are on their own is crucial. Without any immediate pressure on them, and with the security of trusting their teacher completely, their talk is fluid and wideranging, and they sustain it for over half an hour, trying consciously not to digress. Their talk is a vindication of the teacher's intentions and of the whole way she runs her classroom.

Notice the range of functions the language performs. The girls recall perceptions and responses, and articulate them in words:

Sharon   This black stuff, some squirted out
Nicola   Yes and it's got this lovely colour through it like a rainbow
Sharon   And it looked really (?) and when I touched it it was like horrible
Nicola   Yes and on the outside – oh, we're not on about the outside, erm, on the inside all this sort of black liquid runs out and erm
Sharon   Like black soot but erm
Nicola   It's all runny. . . . I didn't think I was going to enjoy it but I quite – it was quite interesting
Sharon   I really enjoyed it

It's the kind of talk teachers might dismiss as 'silliness', or as a stage beginners unfortunately have to go through before learning to be sensible about such things. But, as we've suggested, it may be important for the success of later operations that the child should initially register fully what is there, repeatedly bringing up for contemplation all the interesting and disturbing aspects, as well as the 'relevant' ones, until they are well and truly assimilated.

Sometimes they raise questions their teacher didn't ask:

77

Sharon   Why do you think we need eyelids, Nicola?

Nicola   Well, they're to protect your eyes, erm, like from the dust and your eyelashes are –

Sharon   And you've got all fat round your eyes and that protects your eyes as well, so if you bang your eyes it's all right

This fact, as it happens, was mentioned by the teacher as she was carrying out the dissection, but that doesn't make Sharon's comment mere idle repetition. This isn't rote repetition, but the application of an acquired piece of knowledge in a fresh context: associating the eye fat with eyelids as examples of protection is, for them, a new and illuminating link.

They speculate, using what they have seen and what they know, to deduce what is likely to be the case:

Sharon   I wonder how long your optic nerve is?

Nicola   Well I think it's, it's quite long to go to your brain

Sharon   Yes, it must do, to go from your eyes. Your eye's about – comes to a few inches further down your head

Their language oscillates between being expressive and really objective:

Sharon   This black stuff squirted out . . .

Nicola   . . . in my eye I've got some white then some blue and then black in the middle

Sharon   Pupil – that's just a hole really and the black stuff inside your eye makes it, erm, black

They try out the new technical language:

Nicola   The rainbow – that's quite nice –

Sharon   The retina

Nicola   Yes, that's what it's called

They experience the excitement and power of illuminating explanations, telling them to themselves to appreciate their full force:

Sharon   When you see what you're seeing is, you're looking at a candle you see blurred and it goes to your eye then it goes through your optic nerve then to your brain then your brain tells you what it is. It says, like, that's a candle. . . . It must go very quick if you can see it straight away

And they ask questions of considerable interest which they can't even begin to answer themselves:

Nicola   What I don't understand, in the bull's eye was that we've got – in my eye I've got some white, then some blue and the black in the middle

Sharon   You've not got black in the middle, it's a hole, it's a hole

Nicola   Yeah well, that's my eye. But that bull hasn't got, erm, or the cow it hasn't got white in its eye

Sharon   I don't see why cows need er eyes because they don't, they, they know where the grass is, don't they, by sniffing

Nicola   Yes and erm I asked Mrs Minns do they know that grass is called grass and Mrs Minns goes 'no' so why do they need eyes? They can just reach their heads down and eat it. They know where it is, they eat it often enough

If we think of this work in terms of the processes which we said earlier need to go on, we can see the girls thoroughly steeping themselves in the detailed reality of the object they've been studying, mastering the new names, trying out the explanations, and putting the knowledge to use to satisfy their own curiosities. And in doing what they need to do as learners, they're providing Mrs Minns, when she plays the tape, with the insights she'll need as a teacher if she is to help them further.

II

A teacher of eleven-year-olds wanted his pupils to learn how to use books efficiently for research. He felt that the way 'project' and 'topic' work normally occurred didn't encourage this: instead, pupils tended to copy and to take easy ways out. So he introduced A–Z books. He gave each pupil a small exercise book (small, so that they would be able to fill it easily). On page 1 they each wrote their own double-column alphabetical list, of things they would like to know more about, with one item for each letter: these would become the titles of the sections of the book. One looked like this, for instance:

Apes	Jam	Socks
Bananas	Kings	Tables
Castles	Lemons	Umbrellas
Dogs	Milk	Vans
Eels	Newts	Windows
Fish	Octopuses	X-rays
Garden flowers	Post	Yachts
Hedgehogs	Queens	Zoos
Ice-cream	Roads	

Then, using these headings as guides to their reading, they set out to complete their A–Z books. At the same time the teacher introduced them to the notion of copyright: he showed them the standard note in all published books: 'No part of this publication may be reproduced . . . in any form or by any means . . .' and suggested that this applied to them, and that they should take great care that whatever they wrote should be entirely their own. The children then worked on their A–Z books during topic-work sessions.

In that first example, the two girls were using talk to speculate and to learn. But reading and writing are the two language modes which education seems to consider the most important. Despite the dominance of these two modes, it's been notable how little has ever been done, especially above the age of seven or eight, to help pupils to learn how to use and control reading and writing, nor to discover how they can be ways of learning rather than simply ways of acquiring or presenting decontextualized chunks of information. Behind the disarmingly simple idea of the A–Z books lies a complex network of possibilities and implications which a thoughtful teacher can explore.

As pupils devise their lists of contents, they are focussing in on a kind of 'feature list': depending on how the A–Z is initially framed, they will be able to identify particular features of topics which catch their interest. Thus, beginning with a selection from the whole universe like the A–Z already shown, with Socks and Queens, we can narrow it down to animals, and the pupils begin to subdivide. Their lists look like this:

Ants	Ibis	Queen bee
Birds	Jaguar	Rabbit
Cats	Kangaroo	Skunk
Dogs	Lion	Turtle
Elephant	Mouse	Unicorn
Fish	Newt	Vole
Goat	Octopus	Whale
Horses	Polar bear	Zebra

Focus in still further, and we get a boy's A–Z on horses, which begins 'Arabian; Bay; Curry comb . . .' A sixth-former studying English was invited to compile an A–Z on the work she was having difficulty with – Ted Hughes's poetry. Her list took her over a week to compile, and began 'Anger; Blackness; Cruelty; Destruction; Egotism'.

Devising the A–Z list is itself, then, a useful focussing device by which a learner begins to see what he or she understands, and how much is known already. But it does more than that: it helps a learner to 'frame' a task. The term 'framing' was coined by Tony Burgess *et al.* (1973). He talks of the writer faced with the problem of knowing where and how to begin, and suggests that the writer

> can construct a framework within which the task can be fulfilled, which . . . limits the space which is to be occupied, but, at the same time, enables the possibilities which can go on within it. Out of the link which the writer makes between a situation, which is given from without, and his resources and experiences of language within, he *frames* his task, sets up for himself the limits and possibilities within which his search for meaning can take place. (p. 15)

Framing is, as anyone who has ever had to write will know, the central demanding problem of writing. When students say to their teachers, 'I don't know what to write', they generally mean 'I don't know how to begin'. The A–Z is one way of framing: by the time learners have identified the topic, they have gone a long way towards framing it, too. The sixth-former doing English found that by the time she had finished her contents list she had both begun to sort out her ideas to the point where she was able, for the first time, to write about Hughes: she had delimited her topic in a way that made it manageable.

The A–Z may appear a rather frivolous device. Certainly, to allow initial letters to determine your field of operations introduces an arbitrariness which goes against the serious academic grain. But this is the *first-draft* stage of learning, the stage in which 'lateral thinking', even play, are entirely appropriate. At this point in learning, such an unpressured form of writing is exactly what is required: the length of the pieces can depend on how much the writer finds there is to say. The control by writer rather than teacher over what exactly shall be written enables peculiar and unexpected directions to be followed. (Zest in Ted Hughes? There is energy, and appetite, but why doesn't 'zest' seem right?) Moreover, underlying the A–Z are two sound principles which apply, whether or not this particular ingenious technique is employed: first, that you can only come to grips with a subject by engaging with its detail – the A–Z gets you off the bank and into the water; and, second, that you need to take a three-dimensional view of a topic and ask diverse sorts of questions in order to get an adequate conception of it.

One final point about the writing. Because the learners define the topics and how they shall be written about, the writers' relationship with their audience changes. Instead of writing for teacher-as-examiner, they are writing as expert-to-layman, or to teacher as trusted adult: it is the pupil who knows, and the teacher who is to learn from what the writer says. The effects on the pupils' writing can be dramatic.

III

Nicola and Sharon were talking; the students doing the A–Z were reading and writing. As we move up the age-range we find the students writing more and more, but, curiously, the varieties and the range of functions of the writing do not expand but actually diminish (Britton *et al.* 1975). The uses of writing which, judging by the examples quoted, seem to take the students forward in their learning seem to be those in which the writers are discovering something for themselves at the same time as they tell it to others. As students get older, what opportunities are there to use writing to this effect?

Stephen, a twelve-year-old boy, was at the beginning of his second year in comprehensive school. In his Religious Education lessons over three weeks, he did these three pieces of writing which he still remembered vividly a year later.

Man the thinker

Man is superior to animals because he thinks about things, and asks the questions how and why. His curiosity asks questions quicker than he can answer them, so there are hundreds of unanswered questions. Here are some of them:

Is there a Loch Ness monster?
Is there a Bigfoot?
If there is a god, who created him?
When will the world end?
Why are there wars?
Why are there different kinds of religion?
How do birds find their way while they are migrating?
Why are people violent?
Are there any ghosts?
Why do some people grow tall and some people stay small?
How did the earth begin?
Is there a Yeti?
Is there life on other planets?
Will we ever go to a planet outside the solar system?
Will there be a world war 3?
Why was Stonehenge built?
Can anything travel faster than light?
Will there be another saviour?
Why is there nature?
Were there any dragons?
When did man discover fire?
Is there a heaven and hell?
What came first, the chicken or the egg?
Did Atlantis exist?
How many elements are still to be discovered?
Can plants 'see'?

Some of these questions will be answered in the near future, but some will never be answered. And forever, man will be asking these questions.

Awe

Halfway up a mountain, the giant object silhouetted against the bright sky. The great reaches of a lake distant down below. Minature trees reflect the blazing sun which peeps out from behind powdery clouds. The green grass sprouts up from the soft peaty ground. The air smells so fresh. Gently rolling hills give way to craggy rugged mountains as if they are young and the peaks are by far their senior. One can almost imagine beards hanging from the rocky crags. Green fields hazy and unreal, filled with specks of colour that are the flowers. All of this view is a credit to nature. It is this kind of thing that inspires poets and artists who notice this beauty of nature and are sensitive to it.

Do ghosts exist?

For
1 People who have just seen them look frightened.
2 Unexplained things have happened.
3 Ghosts are seen by someone who doesn't know that the person is dead.

Against
1 No scientists have seen them with their equipment with them.
2 No absolute proof.
3 People have been caught playing tricks.

This work is interesting in two ways: for what it shows of one particular teacher's approach, and for what it suggests about the total experience of a pupil in one of our schools. At the same time as he was writing these pieces in RE Stephen was, of course, writing in all his subjects. In geography, for instance:

Growing coffee on the Fazenda do Bosque
The coffee seedlings are planted four to a hole. These holes are at fixed intervals and are filled with fertilizer. If the land is sloping contour ploughing has to be used. This is ploughing round in a circle so that you are on the same level all the time. This stops the very heavy rains running away with the precious earth. When the plant is fully grown it is about 9 feet high.
(Pencil drawing of 'Branch of coffee plant')
The beans are picked by hand and are either passed through a pulping machine, allowed to ferment and washed to remove the pulp; and dried, or dried in the sun for days or weeks, and have the outer husk removed. Then it is graded and tested.

In English:

Night and morning

1   In the autumn night the moon is low on the horizon and the dusk covers the ground like a blanket miles thick. In the morning, the frost covers trees and grass and the air is foggy and clammy.
2   In passage no. 2 I am conscious of more sounds.
3   The greatest range of colour is found in passage 2. In passage 1 the colours are mostly dark blue and black.
4   Passage one seems stiller and I would paint it with no people in it.
5   Passage 1 has more details, like when the author describes the sheaves of hay or corn. They add more to the picture of the scene like adding pieces to a jigsaw.

In maths:

*AR. C.*6

1   12 cm^2
2   12 cm^2
    This is because the triangle on the left is the same as the one on the right.
3   Because the triangles are the same.
4   No, he measured the line instead of measuring the height.
5   a) 8 cm^2
    b) 6 cm^2

And so on in all his subjects. Now, there is nothing intrinsic to any one subject that says that the writing in it shall or shall not be of interest to the writer, or to whoever reads it. What determines this seems to be not the subject but the teacher and the terms in which he or she sets up the writing for the pupils. Nowhere else does Stephen's writing show the same engagement, the interest in what he's doing, or the concern for spelling and handwriting that it does in RE. He cared about what he was writing, and, judging by the way he spoke of it a year later, he evidently learnt from the writing and continued to think about it long afterwards.

There has always been discussion about whether 'subjects' have particular forms of written language which inevitably attend them. If one asked what kind of writing is appropriate to RE, it's hard to see what answer would be most common among

85

those who teach it. But this particular RE teacher has deliberately generated *varied* forms of writing in his pupils: and what is particularly striking is that although every child was writing to the same topic the topics were open enough for all the children to find something of their own to say, drawing on their own stories of memories and experiences. Thus the invitation to depict 'Awe' enables Stephen to make something from his images of the mountains which he loves.

The geography piece is, of course, a competent job; its structure and clarity, and the expressive word 'precious', suggest that it was carried out in a far from perfunctory spirit; the teacher would be justified in feeling satisfied with it. But it is not, like the first two RE pieces, a direct expression of and means of working on issues and experiences that powerfully preoccupy the writer. Nor, of course, is it meant to be; the task in hand is learning about coffee. Nevertheless, it would be a mistake to think that the nature of geography-learning inexorably dictates that the writing must be of this kind. If, for instance, one were to broaden the 'frame' of the topic so as to include not only the processes of cultivation but the lives of the cultivators, and the meaning of coffee to them (as, for instance, a crop they grow entirely for consumption by people richer than themselves in other countries richer than theirs), then all sorts of wider speculation and imagination become possible, bringing with them, into the arena of the geography lesson, some of the student's deeper interests and motivations. By thus expanding the area in which the student can operate, and making it possible for him or her to mobilize imagination and past experience for the understanding of the topic, a teacher would not be diluting the attention given to the cultivation process itself but enhancing it by locating it in a comprehensible human setting. Because new and varied kinds of understanding would now need to find expression, working like this would inevitably result in Stephen using more varied kinds of writing. Perhaps then the result would be that he would be able to find the same kinds of opportunity to let his voice and enthusiasms be heard that at the moment he only finds in Religious Education. And perhaps, too, that would commit him more to his personal engagement with the concepts and ways of thinking that the subjects offer him as he progresses through school.

IV

As students become older and especially as they pass the age of statutory schooling, it is taken for granted that they are now more willing learners, that they increasingly see the point of what they are doing, and are better able to cope with complex ideas. These assumptions may be fair ones; but at the same time, the subjects are getting harder. Adult responses and adult experience may be called on while the students are still adolescent. Literature and poetry especially can be difficult to read at any age, with their intricate structures and their concern with the subtler and less easily articulated areas of experience, but are even more so when the readers are inexperienced, both in reading and in living. Able students embarking on an advanced literature course will still need careful help, as our next example shows.

An English teacher began a unit of work with a sixth-form group of seventeen-year-olds on Keats. Although the students had been comfortable with the novels and plays they had studied, they felt uneasy about reading poetry, and especially poetry from an earlier time. His series of lessons (one lesson of 70 minutes per week for a term) was designed therefore to introduce them to the work of Keats, to show them how to read poetry, and to raise some questions, obviously important to their course, about the basic processes of reading. He dealt with each of the poems that they studied in a different way, and made explicit on each occasion the basic reading and learning processes that he felt were going on. Thus, the students themselves were always made aware, before the work, of the intentions that lay behind it.

Among the various strategies he used, these were some:

1 He asked them to keep a logbook throughout the course. Every time they read any of Keats's work, they were to keep the logbook handy, and jot down their thoughts. This logbook would remain private to them, and they need not ever show it to the teacher, unless they wanted to.

2 With 'Ode to Psyche', the students were in small groups of two or three, each group with a tape-recorder. They talked their way through this first encounter with the poem, and later, in their groups, wrote down one interesting comment someone else in the group had made, and something they had said themselves that they wanted to remember. Later, they

transcribed the two or three minutes of talk from the tape that they thought were most interesting.

3 He recorded a reading by Sir Ralph Richardson of 'Ode to a Nightingale', and played it to the group, line by line. As they heard it, they wrote down a prose meaning of the words that satisfied them. Afterwards, they discussed the parts they had found most difficult, the interpretations they had made, and whether the poem had been interpreted by the reader in a way they agreed with.

4 He introduced them to an aspect of reading which everyone 'knows about', but not consciously, when they came to read 'Ode on a Grecian Urn':

Teacher You know, but you've probably never thought about it, that your eye doesn't go straight along the line, does it, word by word. It jumps and stops, jumps and stops and er takes in about three to six words every jump when it stops. When your eye stops that's called – the psychologists call that 'fixating' – fixation, yes? Well, when you read something hard and difficult, you – your eye doesn't – well it fixates, but you backtrack as well, you go back and read it again if you haven't understood it. Well now I want you to be conscious of what your eyes do – it's hard this but what I mean is every time you find you've backtracked stop and write down exactly what's in your head. That's really important – it's got to be just what's in your head, and number each thing you write.

When everyone, including the teacher, had done this, they passed around their papers and read what everyone else had written, and the final meaning they'd made of this poem.

5 The students read 'Lamia' at home. At the beginning of the next lesson, he asked them each to spend twenty minutes writing down questions they'd like to have answered. They shared their questions and talked them through with each other; and before the next lesson, the teacher wrote replies to some of the questions, in a kind of letter to the group.

Much of what is going on here is probably obvious. The main feature is its explicitness, the way the teacher attempted constantly to make clear to the students what it was they were doing, and why. The ability to read and understand complex literature can easily seem a mystery to young learners, a ritual secret that can only be understood by the rite of passage of examination and degree. But here, there is no magic: the mechanisms are put into their own hands, and the teacher has no secrets, no hidden purposes.

Even more telling, though, is the total interaction between all four language modes. There are no occasions when one mode is being operated separately. The logbooks synthesize reading with writing, and in some cases report on talk, when the students comment on discussions. The talk about the 'Ode to Psyche' was underpinned by the constant rereading of the text in front of them; the work on 'Nightingale' involved attentive listening, writing and talking; and so on. The complicated sequence of events involving 'Lamia' would have been even more searching had there been time, as he intended, for him to introduce the students to the literary reference section of the library, for them to see if they could find answers to their questions through research. That would have made four quite separate types of reading; of the poem, of their own and each other's questions, of reference books, and of his letter.

In their talk, the students were constantly making first tentative formulations and discovering, like Stephen in his writing on 'Man the Thinker', that they *could* be tentative, that they did have things to say about Keats's poems, and that what they said was often helpful to others, as they discovered in the session on 'Psyche'. In their writing, they worked towards statements, rather than being expected to make definitive statements in 'essays' straight away. And all the time they were learning about reading, and learning, too, something even more important; that Keats, and perhaps all literature, and maybe even all full, mature knowledge, is difficult, not because they the students were inexperienced, so that one day it would be 'easy'; but because it *is* complex, so that the teacher also found difficulty in understanding it.

Their logbooks remained private, but here for comparison are some brief extracts from the logs of some older students, at a college of education, reading Twain and Hemingway. Their logbooks show that this kind of writing, free from public constraint and external expectation, is a way in which the students could make early ideas explicit to themselves, without needing to give them immediate definitive statement in formal essays:

Student 1

Huck and the woman (Chapter 11) Something has just struck me about this whilst reading this chapter – how much their lives revolve around the river. I realized it when the woman was talking to Huck about her relations down the river and then her relations up the river. How strange that this hasn't hit me before because really all Huck's adventures have been connected with the river.

Student 2

Three stories from *The Snows of Kilimanjaro*, 'Out of Season', 'Cat in the Rain', and 'Mr and Mrs Elliott' have depressed me this morning. The weather is really dismal in the stories and it is also outside. I just had to put the book down it made me feel so miserable.

Student 3

Read to the end of *Huck Finn*. Looked through it again, gave a great deal of thought to the book. Jim worried me a great deal. I felt he was not given much of a chance. He is portrayed as being rather simple – thick. This seems unjust to me. Something is really troubling me, can't as yet realize what it is.

When we consider the questions about 'Lamia' these seventeen-year-olds asked, and their teacher's responses, it's notable that they ask questions that teachers wouldn't necessarily think of asking; but it's also notable that they have so many questions to ask. Conventionally, the asking of questions is something that teachers do, and it's the most powerful way of controlling the direction of classroom discourse, and of exercising controls of several kinds (see Sinclair and Coulthard 1975). When the pupils ask the questions, and the teacher answers them, a very different kind of authority relationship is generated, and a very different approach to the knowledge itself. The questions and answers are not then hurdles in a never-ending examination of the pupils, but part of a search for elucidation and understanding on the part of both learner and teacher. Some of the students' questions are literal ones:

Who was Muses?
Bacchus – God of what?

What are syrops?

But they also ask searching questions that take them to the heart of the poem:

> 'Philosophy (= Apollonius?) will clip an angel's (= Lamia?) wing'
>
> Is Keats saying that philosophy will overpower Beauty?
>
> Moral of the story being? Is union between mortal and immortal, what Lycius aspired to, possible?
>
> It seems that Lamia fears knowledge but why should this be? If she is a woman now, does it matter what she was before? If so why?

Whether or not you, the reader, are familiar with, or interested in the poetry of Keats, it's still clear that these students have begun to tussle with core meanings, not surface literalism. They are displaying that quest for meaning which should be the essence of any advanced course, whatever the subject. And their teacher's response is in the same language – personal, casual, but handling the ideas in the terms established by his students. They will learn as much from the manner of his response as from the substance of it. His response to the middle question above, for instance in the letter he wrote, is this:

> The moral? I've no idea, really I haven't. In one sense, it doesn't need a moral: the reader experiences particular emotions which act upon him or her, and move sympathies one way or another. Who do you feel most sorry for. Apollonius? hardly, even though in a different poem, you might expect him to have felt bad over Lycius. (Keats actually seems to imply he'd have gone off feeling all self-righteous.) Lycius? well, yes but . . . Lamia? well again, yes but . . . There seems to be a difference between who we *ought* to feel sorry for (Lycius) and who we actually *do* feel sorry for (Lycius and Lamia). And I suppose the moral of that is that Keats didn't really have his own loyalties sorted out.

That note of tentativeness, of personal responsiveness, and of trusting in one's own language and responses, is the keynote too of the series of lessons in this chapter. It's an atmosphere that derives not from the 'subject' or the topic being dealt with, but from the style of the teacher, and the search for ways of helping the students to comprehend the intellectually demanding material they are meeting. There is nothing in the intrinsic nature of any school subjects that makes such a climate unattainable.

In these case studies, the language activities that the teachers got the students to engage in evidently enabled thought to move, knowledge to grow or consciousness to develop. But the activities themselves have little in common: sometimes the form is completely open (talk on the tape, keep a log), sometimes it is tightly prescribed, but with no restrictions on content – write down a topic for each letter, note three arguments on each side, pick two minutes of tape. It seems that the variety itself is important: different forms allow different sorts of awareness to come to the fore, and there is a close and reciprocal relationship between the form in which ideas are expressed and the nature of the ideas themselves. What appears to be constant behind these successful practices is a particular sort of climate: without it those open forms may well have remained unfilled, because the pupils would not have been prepared to make use of them. The pupils whose work you have seen chose to use them because the climate that their teachers created encouraged them to make choices and to take seriously their own provisional and tentative opinions.

Looking at learning together

What you have seen so far has shown pupils involved in those processes we have called 'learning'; mastering terms and names; putting the knowledge to use to satisfy curiosity; letting the mind follow its natural directions as well as thinking 'relevantly'; calling up past knowledge and experience, and so on. But we also said earlier in the book that it is important to make explicit to the students how they themselves can learn to control the processes of language by which they learn. This involves a consciousness of self which students are unused to: they do not often have it made explicit to them that psychologists suggest that the threshold of attention is only about twenty minutes; that when reading lasts for bursts of only a minute or so at a time it is hard to understand (Lunzer and Gardner 1979); that it is far easier to learn from your own formulations in language than from dictated notes (Howe 1977); that not everyone writes by making detailed plans beforehand, and that, anyway, you can only make such plans when you know what you want to write.

Yet even if children are not familiar with these ideas, they 'know' them in a different way, because they have had experience, every day of their school lives, of how they, personally, work. And when they are consulted they are perceptive, helpful and generous in what they say. They can advise us, if we listen to them, on general aspects of our teaching:

My thoughts on writing are we should write three days a week on plain paper. The comments on the bottom should be obeyed even though I don't always do as it says, because there only to help you work better. The work should not be marked every time only when the child wants them marked, and the only people to look at them are the teacher if the child let's them and the child. The child should be allowed to talk and do as less or as much as they like. They should be able to do what they like in writing and not be

told what to do. The pens should be given by the school.
The best time to do Topic is on Monday and Tuesday. If
they want it on the wall they can but if they don't it must be
left down. The date does not have to be put on if the child
dosnt want to.
(Boy, 12)

They can let us know clearly how they feel, and in doing that,
signal back to us what we are doing:

I do not like story very much. I have not liked any of the
stories on the radio. I quite like poems. But I think it is
good to write a poem or a story because you use your
imagination. I do not like copying stories from the radio.
I like it better if somebody tells you you must write about
spring or something like that. I think it is good to mark
spelling mistakes, and the beginning of a sentence. I do
not like topic at all. Because we have to say what they have
put in the book we are working from in other words. I am
scared if somebody reads my story out because I think it is
not very good.
(Girl, 11)

I don't like writing when I am hot and I don't mind writing
when I am cold when I write in hot weather I get headeck
I don't feel like writeing much now because I have just come
back from danceing and that makes me very hot. I don't
mind writeing when I know what I am going to right but I
tend to work bad when I don't know.
(Girl, 11)

When I write it is as if all the ideas in my head have come
together into order and when I write I am reading them for
the first time.
(Girl, 13)

We can discover that something we have always taken for
granted doesn't apply at all to many of our pupils. Does everyone enjoy having work read out or displayed? Some do:

I enjoy creative writing. I don't mind reading my work out
to the class. I am not embarrassed when I read my work out.

I like seeing my work on the wall and I wish every bit of my work could go on the wall. I certainly don't want my work kept in my desk so that only I can see it.
(Girl, 9)

But others very definitely don't:

I would like to have my parents only see my work because I think they can juge my work better than the teacher I don't like somebody else looking at my work.
(Boy, 9)

I think my work is terrible because when I listen to other people read there's it always seems to be better than mine.
(Girl, 9)

I don't like reading my work out because I don't want to tell everyone what I have wrote.
(Boy, 9)

They can see the relationship between their work, the way they are judged, and their view of themselves. Indeed, these comments by children on their own school experience demonstrate the importance of self-regard, not just to learning in school, but to everyone's total image of themselves. When we pay attention to these comments we are truly paying attention to the 'whole child'. As the girl shows us in the next comment, what to the teacher is a job of work, is for the pupils a far more serious and far-reaching experience.

I enjoy reading to me reading is intresting when I was young I could not read as well as the other children to them I use to be the class dunce. but as I came into a new class a cind teacher by the name of Mrs Jones decided that she was going to bring me up to date with my work when the end of the year came I could not bare to leave my class or teacher she had been good and cind to me. Now I was a child how would not be ashamed to talk about my work and was proud to be able to read and write a lot better. Now I am on library books I enjoy them very much the reasson is because when I read a feeling of sadness and happyness go's through my mind and body making sound unhearable the onley things

I can see or hear are the things that are in the book when I am reading. I can think of the things I need to think about like my work and I think thats the reasson I like reading.
(Stephanie)

Other comments, if we invite them, can show us serious problems that are so obvious that teachers often just don't see them:

What's the use of giving me homework when I can't do the classwork?
(Girl, 15)

They can understand in the most gratifying way things we might feel are too subtle and sophisticated for them:

Mrs X's lessons are really good. You have these big discussions and really you don't think you're learning anything, but at the end of the lesson you know ever so much more than you did before.
(Girl, 14)

When you started us working like this I hated it. All this having to decide what we were going to do, I wished we were in Mr X's class, he tells them what to do. But I think weve learned more than them now, and theyre all saying how boring he is.
(Boy, 14)

And we can learn about the effects of our behaviour. A group of twelve-year-olds, discussing teachers, said:

Teachers won't really listen to you. They've always got half an eye on what everyone else is doing. I was talking to Miss X and in the middle of it she walked off and told these other kids off. I felt really silly.

Can we afford not to seek and take note of feedback like this? If we invite learners to speculate on their own experience of being taught, or of reading and writing, they can teach us about the relationships and conditions that are necessary to them to work effectively. They need sympathetic attention, the chance to work on the learning at their own pace in their own way, help in organizing and 'framing' tasks which stretch them, and responses that will both signal success and indicate gaps and how work might be improved. One group of thirteen-year-olds, asked what a good teacher was, were quite clear: it's someone who won't snap at you if you get something wrong, helps you over the problem, lets you talk rather than insisting on silence, and makes you interested by being interesting about the subject, and interested in you.

Finally, then, putting together our slowly-acquired understandings of our pupils, of the way language works, and of the kinds of context that best assist learning, we may be in a position to design activities that will help our students to become conscious of and to control those basic language processes that will be asked of them throughout education. But the students must see that what they are learning is not just techniques for playing the school game – how to write essays for teachers, how to study and revise for exams – but for learning and studying in any circumstances, in school or out. What is learnt on specifics should be generalizable to a world in which writing and reading and problem-solving discussions will be used as a matter of course; the language of school should also be a language for life.

The following case studies, then, are of teachers explicitly examining with their students three activities that are basic to most school work: how to write formal, 'public' essays; how to research and write projects; and how to synthesize existing knowledge with new demands.

Essay writing: Mussolini's rise to power

Most students find formal essay writing is difficult. They are not certain how to organize an essay, how to decide on what to include or omit; they are uneasy about style and tone, because they may not be quite certain what they're supposed to be doing, and hover uneasily between copying chunks out of books, and not using books at all. The 'essay' of course, is a form that hardly exists outside formal education; but it still controls examination classes. Moreover, there are good arguments for some kind of formal presentation, essay or something like it: the ability to marshall and organize information that one wishes to present to readers, is a highly desirable one.

But that makes it clear why essay writing is so hard. One can only really write an essay successfully when one understands the material sufficiently to be able to select from it, organize and classify it. Too often, though, students are expected to write essays as a way of coming to understanding, but then have the essay assessed as though it were the *product* of understanding. Clearly, this is unhelpful to learners. How can they be helped to learn about essay writing in a way that will support and encourage their learning? In the example that follows, we see a teacher trying to do exactly that.

A history teacher started his fifth-year group on the essay title 'Explain why Mussolini rose to power in the years up to 1921'. He told them they would be working on this in class for the next four lessons (of 70 minutes each), and that they would be using the lessons to explore how best to write essays. They were to work in small groups of three to four and could, if they wished, produce a group essay at the end.

They began. After fifteen minutes, he stopped them and asked them what they were doing. Each group, it appeared, was writing down everything it knew, or could glean, about Mussolini in essay form: they had started, in other words, to write the essay. 'Is what you've written all directly relevant to the title?' he asked. No, they said, and added that they generally found it difficult in most subjects to write essays that were.

He presented them with three questions to help them control their material. Holding in mind the idea of 'Mussolini's rise to power', they were to ask, *What do I know already?*

This would enable them to bring into focus their existing knowledge. But it also showed them the gaps, and so the second question was to be: *What do I need to know?*

The groups plotted the kind of question they wanted to find answers to – one group, for instance, wanted to know why the Fascists came into being as they did, and discovered they were also discussing the National Front. Another group said to the teacher, 'We know that these things happened when they did, but *why*? What *made* them happen when they did?'

When they had sorted out what they felt they needed to know, he asked them the third question: *How do I find the answers?*

The teacher offered three possible answers: find someone who knows and ask him; find someone who knows as much as you and talk about it; and use books. He provided them with a table-ful of books from the stockroom – textbooks, 'real' history books, Jackdaws and other materials. The students had to choose which books they thought would help them, using titles, lists of chapter headings, indexes, and then search for the answers to the questions they had asked. They discovered that the books contained deeply conflicting information. But their noting down of the answers to the questions led them to see what the function of note-taking is, and how sometimes they could write down the exact words of the original, sometimes had to reformulate it, sometimes had to summarize a whole section.

As they collaborated, they also had to discuss with each other the value of the information they were collecting and evaluate it before adding it to the pile they had, or discarding it. 'What about this?... Is this any use?... Hey, listen to what I've just found'. And then the hard bit: how to organize all this information, these pages of notes and references?

The whole class discussed what they'd found, and together devised an outline for what the essay might be: not a 'plan': that would be too limiting. It was a loose structure that would help them to 'frame' the task. Interestingly, they all chose to write individual essays. Although the collecting had been collaborative, they felt they had to write as individuals.

A different problem arose here: how to say clearly what was in the head. 'It's hard to say what you want to in words,' said one, 'They don't mean what you want them to mean.' The teacher suggested that they try and draw a diagram of what they wanted to say, showing relationships between the various chunks of information by position on the paper, by arrows, by connecting lines and so on. Once they'd done that, he pointed out that one of the problems of the kind of writing they were doing was interconnecting the ideas, and that the layout on the paper often demonstrates relationships more clearly than words alone could. He showed them an example from some other pupils' work on Celtic settlers in post-Bronze Age times, where a group had produced, as part of a diagram, this:

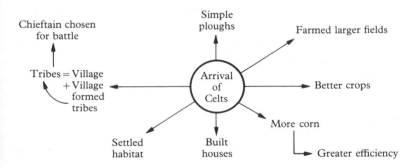

The students realized that the diagram can be described in words in several different ways. It presents all the information simultaneously, and as it is considered, an organization can begin to form in the mind: that organization brings with it ways of expressing the relationships in language. Connectives such as 'consequently – therefore – at the same time – moreover – however' grow out of the perceived relationship between ideas.

Finally, he pointed out that although, as their history teacher, he inevitably knew more about Mussolini than they did, he didn't know anything about the particular perspectives on Mussolini they had discovered, nor what their final conclusions were. About those, they were the experts, and should write as such to inform him. He didn't want to be told back what he'd told them, nor, directly, what the books said: he wanted their unique, personal interpretations supported by the historical research they'd been doing. In saying this, he was changing and making explicit the kind of audience they were to write for. At the end of the fourth lesson, he asked them to write their essays at home.

What the students will have consciously learned in this series of lessons is interesting enough: how to collect information, select what is appropriate and reject what is not; organizing it into different patterns and perceiving the corresponding shifts in emphasis this would bring to the essay; and discovering the relationship between what they knew and felt and what their reader wanted to know. But there were other things being learnt here, too, which would reinforce and be reinforced by, all the other history lessons they had had. They compared primary and secondary sources, and had to evaluate them; they discovered differing interpretations and had to decide which seemed most probable; they discovered a personal point of view based entirely on the evidence they had collected. And finally, they discovered from their teacher what it means to take a historical topic seriously and to begin to see its full implications. In other words, because the teacher set out to demystify a process of education, and made them into partners in the exploration, the students became more committed learners.

Project work

A humanities teacher with a fourth-year group was worried that 'projects' frequently consisted simply of information, copied or paraphrased from books. He looked for forms of writing that would encourage and allow thinking *about* the knowledge, and would let the students express the full range of their responses to the topics. In explaining his proposed format in this handout, he invited the students to think for themselves about the processes of learning, and of education.

How To Do A Project

Many projects are a dead loss because they're nothing more than information from books or pamphlets. Who'd want to read them when they could go to the books or pamphlets and get it straight from the horse's mouth?

These projects seem to be pretending to be books – all about transport, history of fashion, etc, etc. But books are to *inform* people who are going to buy them or get them out of libraries. Projects aren't for that at all – they're a way for *you* to learn. So why write them as if they're phoney second-rate books? (Whoever saw a book written in biro?)

These projects-pretending-to-be-books aren't any good for CSE or GCE assessment either, because they don't show that you know anything or have thought about anything. The only ability they demonstrate is the ability to put other people's words into different words – when the other people's words were probably perfectly all right to start with.

So:
These suggestions are for the purpose of making projects more useful.
To follow them, you need to understand something about different sorts of writing.

1   BOOKS are written to be read by anybody. That's why they're written the way they are. The man writing the book doesn't know who's going to read it or where or when. The audience he's addressing is the public. And he's addressing them for a very clear purpose – to tell them things he thinks they'll want to know.

2   You know more or less who your readers are going to be – your tutor, maybe some other people in your year,

an assessor. When you're writing to someone you know you don't write the way book-writers do. You know you can just be yourself and you don't pretend the whole world is going to read your words. Think of the writing you do in your logbooks, those of you that use the log as a way of talking to your tutor. Some of the best writing that gets done is in logbooks – because it's honest and relaxed.

3   Sometimes you write only for yourself. That's a different sort of writing again. Say you're making notes on a book, and you know the only person those notes will be useful to is you, later. You won't need to spell everything out, you can use symbols and abbreviations and shorthand. This is writing for an 'audience' of yourself.

Now to your project. Let's say you've already got together the books, etc that you need. Here's how to organize it.

HAVE THREE SECTIONS.
START SECTION 1 AND SECTION 2 AT ONCE.
START SECTION 3 LATER.

The differences between the sections are that they are written for different 'audiences'.

Section 1
Audience: your tutor – a particular person whom you know and who knows you, so you won't be writing as if you're writing a book. It will be more like your logbook. Your teacher will write back and you will have a sort of correspondence.

Start Section 1 by telling your tutor why you want to do the project and what you want it to be about. Tell him the sort of things you know already about the topic and the sort of things you'd *like* to know. Say how you think you'll go about it, i.e. map out your plans. Say what problems you can see coming up. Ask any questions you want to. Say how you *feel* about starting the project.

From then on, write in Section 1 very frequently. Make it a running commentary on how your project's going, what you're thinking and what you're learning. You'll be talking to your tutor but at the same time you'll really be talking out your own thoughts for yourself. His replies should help you along.

Ask questions; note down ideas for things you might do later; record your reactions to the material; let off steam when you get frustrated; think up theories and explanations; talk about worthwhile things you're learning; record any changes in your original plan.

(Although it's personal between you and your tutor, the assessor will see this section. From it he'll be able to learn a lot about what you've got out of the project, and what you've put into it.)

Section 2

Audience: yourself.

This section is your *notes* on the books etc you're using. This is where you record any information you need to record. It should be in *note* form, arranged on the page in shapes that help you to understand the material at a glance. It should not be in continuous prose.

Full references should be included to the sources – author and title of book, date of publication, page numbers.

Also in this section would go any other writing which isn't *mainly* intended to be read by someone else – ideas you want to note down, reminders to yourself, questions that occur to you.

In many *bad* projects the information *is* the project. In *this* method it's only one part. An assessor *will* be interested in it, but he'll be just as concerned about what you've done with the information once you've got it and how you've gone about getting it and what thoughts you've had about it – and he'll learn about those from the other two sections.

Section 3

Audience: public.

It isn't actually going to be published but write it as if it were. It *may* well be seen by other students and teachers, and some projects do get typed out and circulated.

This section will contain polished, well-presented, worked-over, public writing (if it *is* writing – it can be other media such as tapes). In it *you* have to be saying something yourself – not just repeating information you've got from the books. The information may not be original but what you do with it should be. What you've learnt should be put to use, not just written out.

You may want to do one single big piece of work for this section or a collection of pieces. You can include stories, poems, and other fictitious writing, imaginary arguments and letters, reports, leaflets to push through letterboxes – or you can write a book. That's OK as long as it's a *real* book, that provides something for the reader that he can only get from you and *couldn't* get in a better way from other books.

Obviously you need to know a bit before you start Section 3, but you need to be thinking about what will be in it from quite early on. Record your thoughts, ideas and plans in Section 1.

Reading and answering questions

Coping with questions on worksheets and passages to be comprehended is never simple, especially when, as so often happens, the student has to read the passage 'and understand it' and *then* answer the questions which invariably follow. But there are ways of demonstrating how to do this work successfully, and to learn about learning in the process. A geography teacher told his fourth-year class of fourteen-year-olds they were going to do an experiment about how they learned best. The class divided (by drawing lots) into three fairly equal groups, and he explained what would happen.

Group 1 would get the passage and read it, and then receive the questions. Working quite independently, they were to write their own answers to the questions.

Group 2 would receive the questions first, and would have about 10–15 minutes to talk together about them. When they were ready, and asked for it, they would be given the passage, and write individual answers without talking to each other.

Group 3 would have the questions, talk about them, then after 10–15 minutes get the passage. Still in their groups, they would talk their way through the answers, agree on what the answers should be and write the answers down.

Which group, he asked, did they think would do best? They didn't agree, but most thought that either Group 2 or 3 would.

After reading the passage they moved onto the questions, which the teacher had designed very carefully. There were only four; one could be answered fairly easily by reference to the text and the pictures, but some could only be answered by synthesizing what was on the sheet with what they had done previously in geography, or with what their commonsense knowledge and understandings would tell them about the world and about people.

Afterwards, they discussed it together. There was no broad consensus – one girl in Group 1 said she preferred to work on her own and not have to share her ideas – but all of Group 3 said they'd enjoyed it a lot. Group 2 said they'd been glad to have the chance of sorting out what the questions meant together, and wished they'd been able to talk about the answers, too. When the teacher looked afterwards at what they'd written he noted (and pointed out to them) that Group 3 hadn't answered as many questions, but that what they'd done was longer than the other groups' writing, and was expressed more personally: in addition, they had seen more implications, and called on more ideas than the other groups had. Group 1 had answered the more literal questions quite well, but had given up on the more complex wideranging questions. In the discussion, they considered how together they could adjust the sort of work they were doing in geography; they said, for instance, that they felt it was important to be able to talk to each other, but that it was also important to hear what the teacher had to say about it, sometimes before and sometimes after their talk. Finally, they said they didn't mind having notes dictated to them, as long as they could have time to talk to each other about what they meant, and have the chance to ask the teacher questions too. They also took the point the teacher made, when he commented on how different it is to read a passage with questions in mind that you're trying to find answers to, than when you're reading it without knowing why, or what kind of things you'll have to find in it.

By themselves, the specific initiatives which were taken by those three teachers will have brought about only limited changes in the overall effectiveness of students' learning. But they suggest a whole approach to teaching and learning which, if it were to become more general, would result in very noticeable improvements. The approach is simply to make the nature of teaching and learning part of the content of the lessons. These teachers no longer wish to keep the mystery to themselves: instead, they seek to collaborate rationally with their students, drawing on everything that both parties know to devise the most fruitful learning arrangements. Since the hope is that our students will continue to learn after school when there is no teacher to guide them, it seems appropriate that they should be made conscious of how the process works. And since we have already seen that one of the prime conditions for learning is that the learners should feel that they have in some sense chosen to participate in the proceedings, then consulting them about aims and methods can only increase their willing commitment to the work.

That is the justification at a general level. There is also a more immediate and specific reason for putting problems of learning on the explicit agenda of lessons. The normal school experience of specialized forms of writing – essays and reports on one hand, literary forms like story and poem on the other – is of two kinds. Either there is exposure to the form through reading, or there is a regular demand made to write in those forms. And for most students, both these fail to help them to acquire competence in writing. The problems of writing an essay on a topic involve more than simply understanding the knowledge: there also needs to be a conscious focus on the form and process of the writing. Nor is it possible for teachers to provide universal guidelines, or a few curt precepts: there is no one way of writing. Each writer has to discover his or her own way of writing, helped by someone who knows enough about the *process* of writing to show what kinds of thing work: how to get started, how to unblock a logjam, how to organize. The teacher has to be the craftsman who can show the apprentice how to cope; and this cannot be a process of direct instruction, but must involve some sort of cooperative working through by students and teachers together, in which the aims of the activity and the means of achieving it are part of the normal discussion of the classroom. Thus once again we find that relationships between teacher and learner represent not merely a social dimension, incidental to the cognitive process, but are actually structural to that process.

Writing as final presentation

Because the process by which students make sense of knowledge for themselves is so important, the forms of talking and writing discussed so far have mostly been ones designed to allow learners to go over knowledge in their own way, dwelling on aspects that interest them, skimming over ones that don't, without pressures to observe a standard form or produce something finished; in other words, language forms that are appropriate to the early stages of learning. But the teacher's need to get a fair sample of the learner's knowledge for evaluation is a real one, and students don't remain at the early stage. There comes a point when they could with profit set out their knowledge in a more public way.

Traditionally, the solution has been the essay, or the series of written answers of a paragraph or less in length. In fact, these forms have not only been employed for the final stages, in some subjects they have comprised the entire writing output. Writing which merely replicates information, like Stephen's on the cultivation of coffee, seems to serve the teacher's need rather than the student's: but it is doubtful whether the teacher gains much either. Although what such writing displays may in some sense be said to be the student's knowledge, it gives no hint as to what is *not* known, all the associated areas in which there may be confusion: when one is asked in effect simply to write a string of true statements about a subject, it is easy to remain silent on the things about which one is unsure. Indeed, such writing actually encourages concealment, hardly an educationally desirable effect. Moreover, the purpose of the task is not generally one that motivates students. Learners rarely use their powers of organizing and marshalling material and ideas when what they are doing is displaying to a single reader who already knows it knowledge that both writer and reader know is displayed elsewhere. The necessary condition for pulling off a complex exposition, asserting emphases and acknowledging side-issues, while moving the whole thing forward in a definite direction, is that there should be a strong sense of overall purpose – of wanting to say 'This is how it is', so that others can see it. Lacking such an impelling purpose, students write badly and teachers fail to get a true reading of their understanding.

A convention of school writing to display knowledge is that it should be written as if for general publication, and not as a private communication to the one person who will actually read it. So the following piece represents a violation of that convention, but one that the teacher was happy to encourage: the writer acknowledges his real audience.

> I think that Amos was doing the right thing in a way but when he discovered people were listening to him he thought he had power over the people, such as you said in second and third year assembly he cleansed himself above other men, he took his power and started insulting people with it, such as this as it is written in the Bible (page 741, Amos 6 chapter 1) (*quotation follows, ending 'you cows of Busham'*) It is a wonder the rich who had to take such insults should stand for it, and did not call in the law at this time.
>
> But I have my doubts whether this would have had any effect for referring to the Bible again (Amos 5, page 740, 10–12) They hate him who reproves in the gate and they abhor him who speaks the truth. If he had not thrown these insults I would have agreed with him wholeheartedly. For there is too much crime too much noise, hurry polution, he tried to put this right.

It is hard enough for many children to utter at all when their addressee is not physically present, as is the case when they write. To have to write then not even for an absent but known person, the teacher, but for an audience of everybody and nobody, impossible to envisage as a responsive interlocutor, presents problems of what are evidently – judging by the level generally achieved – insurmountable proportions.

In demanding such writing we neither produce accomplished writers nor obtain the evidence we need about what the students are making of the subject. Partly we persist out of a sense that there are certain forms which are appropriate to particular disciplines: but what is appropriate for adult practitioners communicating new knowledge to other practitioners may not be so for learners communicating to a teacher their understanding of established knowledge. Moreover, the experts themselves by no means confine themselves to unexpressive and impersonal exposition with passive verbs, no 'I' or 'you' and an avoidance of everyday words. Is this or is it not respectable science writing?

> The non-mathematician is seized by a mysterious shudder-ing when he hears of 'four-dimentional' things, by a feeling not unlike that awakened by thoughts of the occult.

A science teacher might protest at a student's essay which began like that. Perhaps that would be right: Einstein was a bad student. But if the adults feel free to move outside the conventions, as Einstein does here (Einstein 1960) we should perhaps feel no less inhibited, and by the same token allow students to write with a sense of genuine communication. Professional scientific writing, as we might find it in specialized journals, and indeed the public writing of the research com-munity in general, has been developed since the early days of the Royal Society for a very particular purpose, that of com-municating facts, observations, hypotheses, arguments and so on, with a precision and lack of ambiguity which make possible decisive confirmation or refutation by other members of an expert group. That is not at all the purpose of most school students of science when they write, nor do they have any means of making sense of such a purpose until a much later stage. It does not seem reasonable, therefore, to ask them in the first place to write in those ways, though our long-term aim would certainly be to bring them to see themselves as potential mem-bers of such communities, sharing in those concerns for truth and objectivity.

In the meanwhile, alternatives can be found – once one gets in the habit of asking not 'how can this knowledge be set out?' but 'how can it be put to some use?' The aim must be to avoid the need for hypocrisy on the part of the students: they should not be called on to pretend to be experts addressing the whole civil-ized world when they are still relatively insecure in their learning: what they write should be authentic communications of their own, giving readers something which they could only have got from that writer, even though what it essentially concerns might be well-thumbed knowledge which generations of stu-dents have already sweated through.

The possibilities are enlarged when the use the knowledge is put to can be a fictional one: the writer may imagine being in a different situation with a special purpose. After a field-trip with an eleven-year-old group the geography teacher cast around for alternatives to the standard 'write it up', 'write an account of . . .' task. This was one outcome:

A conversation between myself and someone who doesn't know as much, as we walk along the Cawthorne Dyke

Me   Now then as we come to this place called cawthorne dyke I want you to get prepared well for a long walk. If you have a look on your map. Here we are if you look up there you can see a tree with hardly any land below it. What happened was that the water goes round a bend and it wares away the soil.

Him   But how

Me   Well the bend comes round and the water travels on the outside like a car does, but it goes so fast it just takes the silt with it

Him   Where does it deposit it and it will take over the whole of the field. What is silt

Me   What happens is that when the water gets all the silt it drops it on the other side where the water is slower, so it keeps wearing it away it deposits it on the other side so it forms what we call a horse shoe but the real name is ox bow. Silt is just the soil the muck.

Now then we have come to a valley but there is no stream you see what happens is the sandstone sokes the water up and then when it rains again it comes down further all the other water being held eventually comes out further down in the valley. This is another valley like this the other but the water comes out at different places this is because it depends on how much rain has fallen and how much the sandstone can hold

Him   What happens if it doesn't rain for along time and there is along drought

Me   Well it will just dry out but when it rains it will take alot of rain to get it flowing again

Now then there is a fresh water spring here, can you see the path it made when it gushes down, to stop the water wearing the field away the farmer has put a brick to slow it down.

Him   Why don't we walk lower down down there

Me   Because in winter and in summer if it's been raining alot it will get boggy down there.

This is an old mill if you have a look at the wheel it is about 50 60 feet tall if you see there there is a little pond there is a specail name for this a goit they diverted the water off from the stream then piped it from the goit to the wheel and made it turn the grind stones and the water flowed back into the stream

At one level this may look like just another task, the conventional exercise slightly disguised ('Write a letter to a friend about the Whig Supremacy'). But, given that the writer has decided to accept it and to make the purpose his own, the form has enabled him to do interesting things: he has had to become an active interrogator of the information he knows, and there has been some purpose in his writing as expert. He has been able to *play* with information, to offer definitions of silt, of ox-bow bends, of goit, in a way that gives them a purpose; he has been able to make the information into dialogue. Incidentally he's also been able to explore his own abilities in language: he's asked and answered questions and written play-script dialogue. Thus the teacher's purpose is served as well as the student's: from this writing he can form an adequate impression of what the experience meant to the pupil.

In the same way, would the following piece be an adequate index of a twelve-year-old's grasp of the issues involved in the Opium Wars? What can the teacher learn from the way the writer personalizes issues into human reactions and responses? The writer takes historical information, gives it human voice by dramatizing two points of view, and then brings these two differing points of view into conflict with each other.

A conversacon

1st   Look young fellow I don't care a brass farthing about what you say

2nd   But sir Don't you see all the harm you are doing to the chineses with the opium trade

1st   I make $5\frac{1}{2}$ million pound every year so if you think I'm going to give up that sort of money you got a anther thing coming

2nd   millions of people have died and millions more will

	die if you carry on the opium trade
1st	So what do I care and I'm damed if the chineses care
2nd	Lin Tse Hsu wrote a letter to Queen Victoria.
1st	one chinaman in ten million
2nd	would you sell opium to Englishmen
1st	of course not
2nd	AH Theres my point
1st	most of the swine that would buy it are to full of cheap gin
2nd	opium rots the guts
1st	Gin rots the liver
2nd	I agree but we are discussing the sale of opium to china not the cheap gin that is being sold to the working class
1st	if it was not opium in china it would be some think else
2nd	I agree all socities have some think wrong with them.
1st	so who cares
2nd	Ignorant fool I can see it is silly to argue with you
1st	go then
2nd	I will go back to my gin factory

Admittedly it sometimes takes some ingenuity to think what students can do with a particular bit of knowledge. The material may be interesting and worth while without having obvious applications; yet a written outcome may be necessary for purposes of internal or external assessment, and one wants it to be rewarding for the writer at the same time.

A teacher in a team had a group of students (aged fifteen to sixteen) interested in the organization of displays in supermarkets. He had a lot of inside information on the tricks they use to put the right things in front of the customer at the right points in the circuit. The students ended up very well informed, but what could they do with the knowledge? The task the team came up with was: Imagine you are a supermarket manager who somehow gets inside a rival's premises one night; you set out to rearrange the displays so as to *minimize* your rival's sales next day. Describe what you do.

A sociology course on deviance was drawing to its conclusion. Young offenders, soccer hooligans, drug users and various other groups had been looked at, together with the notions of labelling, the amplification of deviance, 'blowing the whistle' and so on.

The problem was to find a task which would utilize all the new ideas that had been acquired. The solution eventually arrived at was to ask the students (aged fifteen to sixteen) to describe the genesis and development of a new form of deviance:

> . . . As he travelled around, to work and for a drink, people saw him and began to do the same (spreading toothpaste on their navels). Quite soon, great toothpaste gangs began to form. When the gang members were singled out and interviewed, they said, 'It was just to try it out. This bloke talked me into doing it, at first I didn't want to, but then he talked me round and so I did it. There's no harm in it.' But is there? . . .
>
> Stereotypes of toothpaste spreaders formed in 'ordinary' people's minds. They saw the spreaders wearing hipster jeans and shirts tied up round their waists so that everybody could see the toothpaste on their navels. But not all, in fact, hardly any of the toothpaste users or spreaders looked like the stereotypes. . . . The public despised the toothpaste users and this forced them to meet in pubs and cafes, grouping together. They sat in pubs listening to juke boxes full of toothpastie type music. . . . The doctors and police wanted to know whether one brand of toothpaste led to another. . . . Long talks took place between politicians and police officials, who finally decided that a special section of the police force should be devoted to stopping pasties from supplying the toothpaste users with toothpaste. . . . The majority of them said the toothpaste penetrated inside them and gave them a nice, fresh warm feeling inside their stomachs, while on the outer parts of their bodies they had tingling sensations around their elbows, at the base of the neck and behind their ears. . . .

A switch to a different form of writing can sometimes be the means of finding a complete new insight into a subject. No worthwhile 'final writing' really represents a stage *after* learning: in producing the finished statement one is still making discoveries.

In the examples you have just seen – the Opium War dialogue, the supermarket organization, and the deviance piece – students found the topics lively enough to engage them. But the liveliness of the writing should not be allowed to conceal the fact that these are serious and legitimate ways of handling difficult concepts, and they also represent opportunities for students to come to terms with the relationship between complex ideas and their own lives. All subjects pose difficulties as students progress: how, for instance, can a pupil come to understand history? and what does 'understand history' *mean*? It is only as one gets older that one realizes that the past didn't occur as a mass of dates, treaties, battles, and neat, isolated events called 'The Renaissance' or 'The Civil War' or 'The Constitutional Crisis of 1911'. It was what the human world still is: men and women living lives that weave in and out of each other's, sometimes getting caught up by events from outside their immediate environs, events that were generated in some way beyond understanding and that disrupted the 'ordinary' life of the people. At the time we don't explain our lives: we live them. Afterwards, we reminisce, reflect, tell stories, make patterns and meanings – make our own histories and out of them the greater, more intense history that is the interpretation of the past.

Because he was able to choose to write a story about enclosures, a fourteen-year-old boy appeared to feel the humanness of history. Consider what impression the teacher would have formed of the ability of the boy if there had been only the piece written a week earlier to go by:

Speenhamland
In the village of Berkshire in 1795 magistrates gathered for a meeting, they all agreed that relief should be given to agracultural farmers, that are low paid the relief was bread. The came to the conclusion that bread was the most important commodity to live. If there was no bread the family would starve.

Not very distinguished, and no apparent signs of any commitment in the boy to history, or to his own language. But the story he wrote shows him bringing information to life for himself. Despite the anachronisms, and the 'wrong' things, there is a strong feeling of someone gaining an insight into what those times were like.

The decision rests on you
'I thought I told you two to get into bed about half an hour ago! Now go on, I won't tell you again, your mother and I have important business to talk about.'

The children climbed the stairs to bed, and the father sat in his arm chair and said 'I know its a difficult decision to make but it must be made never the less.' His wife sits in dazed thought for a moment before saying 'I'm all in favour of it you know that, but its not just my decision that counts its both of ours.' The man of the house Alfred mumbled, coughed, and then said, 'I don't know, I must be the only man that can't make up his own mind, I sleep on it.'

The next day followed and went just as quick and nothing more was said on the matter, untill there was a meeting where every one was called together to decide weather they should vote to find out if they were going to enclose the village. The final decision was made it was that there was to be a vote. The magistraits were informed, they were due to arrive on 27th of this month which was March.

Alfred and his wife still haddent fully made up their minds, as yet, there was still plenty of time and no need to worry. Talk was going about he was the only one that had'nt made known what his vote was going to be, well he could'nt very well as he himself did'nt know what it was going to be.

The day arrived, everyone marched off to the Town Hall, that was all except Alfred, who the day before had fallen down with flue. An hour had passed and know word had been sent. The waite was to much for him, he got dressed and walked off down the road in the general direction of the Town Hall. He hesitated before entering, the room went sielent, everyone stopped and looked at him. Alfred raised his head and looked at the board at the front of the room, so far the voting had gone all one way, the votes were 64 for enclosure and 12 against. He done a small sum in his head before saying 'It looks like the final decision is mine, if I vote for the 4/5 majority is gained and if I vote against the open field system remains.' Everyone nodded there head in agreement with him. He cleared his throat and said 'My decision is that we should enclose the village.' With this the room filled with chants and cheers. Three weeks later the village was enclosed.

Here is an example to show an alternative possibility in a more specialist field. English teachers in one school, wishing to get away from 'appreciations' and 'comprehensions' as the standard means of writing about poetry, and seeking a form which would allow response rather than prosaic exegesis or criticism, tried what they called 'presentations'. The students would break the poem into chunks and simply write alongside it in what they felt to be the same spirit. The results at least escaped from Robert Graves's 'the thundering text, the snivelling commentary'. Here is the poem 'Whale' by Lola Haskins followed by part of a presentation of it by Wayne who was thirteen.

Like a city bus, white as a new Cadillac,
sudden mountain, surprise from the sea,

A giant sponge, carved marble, grounded cloud, like a wounded hero, albino lung, cold white as a snowdrift, stranded iceberg, bleeding chalk (The first few phrases were written on the board by teacher and class working together.)

Heaving lay on the littered beach
a whale

Wow a whale holy Jack rabbits. Its the first whale I'v ever seen and on our beach. Thats something for the ladies night. It could be dangerous for the boys. 'There playing with it, come away it could kill them'. The tail the Jaw could snap them in half.

and the only sound
was wave-rush in the grey morning
the only sound was fish breathing
faint hiss of water

The only sound was the crackling sand and water mixing together and the cries of children playing in the distance. (Wayne adduces his own experience of beaches – puts it in terms he's familiar with.)

But they found him.
He's not dead, they shouted

Caught him alone, praying for life, lonely hunk of dog food, got time to think, To reflect on his short life, Prisoner waiting for death, Will he be sperd

Too late. Launched, the white whale floated
Like the funeral of all lilies everywhere.

The fight was no good (reference to 'The Fight to Save Our Whale') it flouted like a log. With a trail of white water behind and everone was in morning for the Albino from the sea. And the sea was silent.

In the end he is almost writing a poem of his own. In working on someone else's language, your own creative motor can get kicked into life.

It is not, it must be emphasized, that essays and other 'transactional' writing are empty and pointless: nor are we arguing that students should always be expressing emotions and never writing logically. Our concern is with handling information and ideas, and the argument has been that they get handled more effectively when students are pursuing communicative purposes of their own. In the later stages of learning, the expression of these purposes will take the form of disciplined transactional writing: a mature writer is able to relate not just to single known readers but to a wide unknown audience, and has learnt to value the human search for the truth about the world as genuinely as more personal concerns.

John S, at sixteen, seems to be on the road towards that mature way of participating in the public intellectual life of society. His writing is revealing because it is so clearly transitional, caught somewhere between language for expressing the writer's own thoughts and feelings, and language for displaying the results of thinking in a more public way.

The great demand for land
Very often one here's of how plans are obtained to produce a fantastic new motorway, or perhaps a great Industrial housing estate. But have you ever stopped to consider just how much land a large scale project such as this would involve.

For example, in Britain alone there are 2,000 miles of motorway; this doesn't include the great stretches of minor roads of lesser significance.

Alright, we may need motorways in order to transport our goods, or to enable us to get around. But 2,000 miles of motorway, about 80 to 100 yards wide requires a lot of land. As for housing plans, man cannot live without housing, though the type of house we live in doesn't have to relate to the type of house we require; this point was argued out in a Housing essay I did earlier.

When people plan new housing areas they try to plan so as to produce as many houses on as little land as possible; this may seem to be complete common sense at first view, due to the shortage of land. After all, we have to reserve as much land as possible in order to feed these people. However, Britain still has to import the largest proportion of our food to meet the peoples demands. Importing food whilst great areas of land are being wasted and misused seems senseless to me.

On the following page there is a graph containing the results of a survey I made. For I have already given the planners opinion of how to use land, make compact housing estates and save land for farming. I personally disagree with this, for large areas of land still remain idel even today.

My opinion relates to the people's requirement of food, I wondered just how many people would prefer to grow there own food if given the chance.

Therefore I decided to carry out a survey in order to find out just how many people would be willing to grow there own food.

The results from the 134 houses I visited are on the 2 following pages. The finished result was just as I had expected, an overwhelming majority voted to produce their own food.

Would you be willing to spend hours pleasurably digging in order to produce your own food? I certainly would!

I personally feel that home grown food project could cut Britains food imports, and make better use of Britains idle ground.

(graph and questionnaire tables follow)

Explanation
Personally I think the graph speaks for itself, more than twice the number of people voted to grow there own food; than against it. There were some who would be interested in the idea, if given the chance, there were also people who weren't interested. However, the people who said they hadn't the time confused me. Everyone can find the time if need be, if only people would make that extra effort.

The distance John still has to travel needs no pointing out. But he has already come a long way. He has developed his language to the point where he can put arguments, cite evidence and discuss public issues, largely through pursuing purposes of his own in his own way. He has arrived at this relatively public form not through following a model or observing a convention but because he has found that it objectively meets his needs at the moment. As his needs widen, so the form will develop.

John's comment, 'this point was argued out in a Housing essay I did earlier', is significant. He worked at studies which he chose for himself. The whole opus represents his attempt to comprehend the aspects of society which he found most interesting. In other words, this essay is part of a personal project which is a means of expression for a healthy curiosity and concern: it is school work, but not just school work. That is where the force comes from which makes this achievement possible.

John collected together all the essays which were his final word on the various studies and wrote this at the front of them:

> An essay within a project is basically a summary of the work I have done. Essays also contain my personal views on a particular subject. . . .
>
> Personally I think a project is uncomplete without an essay, or a sum up of ideas. Something which not only contains the facts but also my view on the subject.
>
> Some of the essays which are listed are not necessaryly follow ups to projects, some are based upon simple ideas which I found interesting.

That example shows a student beginning to move towards a more public, impersonal form. The development appears to happen best in the context of an enterprise in which the writer has some personal stake. In John's essay, his involvement as a person is openly acknowledged. Later it will show in the energy of the writing itself. That the production of good transactional writing remains intimately associated with that full commitment – with interest, curiosity and excitement – is revealed in a compelling way by this final case.

A college student was in a group that was shown a loop film of the blood defences: a science lecturer talked them through it, but deliberately in a casual 'non-scientific' way. Afterwards, they wrote about what they had seen but were encouraged to react not intellectually but emotionally. This student wrote a piece, of which this was a part:

> Whilst I was listening to the talk I was thinking how un-scientific and exciting the 'battle of the blood' sounded when put in a non-scientific way, and trying to think how it would have affected my reactions to the tale to have put in cold scientific terms as I imagine scientists, 'real' scientists would do. I'm fairly sure I would have struggled more to understand the process involved in maintaining the body, but I don't think I would have enjoyed it so much.
>
> Have just thought of that marvellous bit of a Tony Hancock TV show about blood doning. Great.

Some time later, she was asked to write about blood in a way that was more scientific. What she wrote gives an unusual glimpse into some of the processes by which new ideas are worked towards, and how writing can grow from the informal 'expressive' form into the public language of formal discourse. But the two remain intimately connected: we do not outgrow the expressive, and then only need the formal. They embody complementary aspects of our thinking, both of which need to be present if we are to engage adequately with knowledge. As they interact and stimulate each other, the learner grows in confidence and in the ability to control and to create order.

Blood
I still can't write about the blood defences in a scientific way. I thought I could and intended writing a strictly factual account using the correct scientific words, and I picked up a textbook.

My heart sank – it all sounded so uninteresting – not at all as I remember it with Angus Stokes. I'd seen the cold dull process they were describing here, and had it explained to me in ordinary everyday language, and it was exciting and interesting. These words meant nothing to me and I closed the book hurriedly and thought back to my private version of blood defences – the red corpuscles doing their bit, quietly fetching and carrying the body's food and waste. Enter the villain – bacteria – intent on destroying and in-vading, followed closely by the hero – white corpuscles siezing them up and eventually surrounding the bacteria and destroying them. . . .

I wrote all this and then I opened the book again and this time I read it and took notes and didn't mind reading it.

Blood is the fluid which carries nourishment to all parts of the body, circulated by the pumping action of the blood. It takes oxygen and certain digestive products to the tissues which need them and takes away waste products which accumulate after severe muscular activity to the excretory organs.

Blood provides the body with its defensive system against bacteria, for white cells congregate round the area bacteria are attempting to invade, surround them, seal the area off, and move in to destroy.

Blood is made up of red blood corpuscles which are suspended in a yellow fluid – plasma. The corpuscles comprise a fine membrane containing a thick red liquid – red because of the pigment called haemoglobin which absorbs oxygen and releases it later where it is needed. When it is full of oxygen and on its way through the arteries it is bright red; on its return through the veins lacking oxygen it is dull. These red blood corpuscles are formed in the bone marrow.

The plasma is made up of water, proteins (which includes a blood-clotting agent) and several salts chief of which is sodium chloride. The white corpuscles are usually larger than the red ones and unlike them contain a nucleus which controls the life and growth of the cell. . . .

I went to the local library and looked for a fairly simple biology book and found one by Patricia M. Kelly called *The Mighty Human Cell*. I haven't read it all but have read enough to see that this book would be very useful to people like me who know little about how our body works in detail. There are lots of diagrams and along with the names of the various cells etc. – e.g. phagocytes – the author gives the pronunciation ('fag-o-sights'). Useful. I learned from this book that phagocytes means 'a cell that has the ability to eat'.

I took a few notes from this book also, and found out that a red blood cell lasts 120 days and during this time travels about 700 miles. It gradually gets damaged as it's pushed along and as it hasn't a nucleus cannot repair itself and eventually bursts.

The liver and the spleen remove the damaged cells from the bloodstream, mash up the cells and save the iron for the body's use (!!)

There are about 400–500 red blood cells to every one white one. The white cells are not alike; there are five different kinds

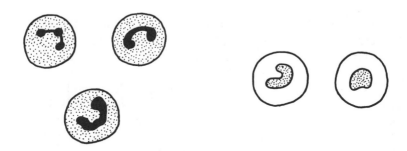

three contain granules in the cytoplasm

Notice also the difference in the shape of the nuclei

Phagocytes – white cells' chief job is to protect other cells against bacteria. They do this in two ways:

1 It puts a 'foot' out like an amoeba and the remaining part flows along to join the foot. In this way the bacteria is surrounded and digested.
2 Some bacteria cannot be destroyed without help and so white blood cells carry an antibody which attacks the bacteria first and it is then digested by the cell. . . .

I didn't intend writing this much but got interested, I hope it's helpful in some way. I certainly feel that if I had been introduced initially to blood and its functions by means of the first textbook I looked at, I wouldn't have bothered to pursue the subject at all.

'These words' she writes about the textbook, 'meant nothing to me, and I closed the book hurriedly and thought back to my private version of blood defences'. Then she reconstructs her initial vivid response, in an attempt to recapture the involvement that first made her interested in the topic. Her writing shows the personal energy of her feelings: 'enter the villain bacteria . . . the hero, white corpuscles . . .' Having done that, the informal writing has served its purpose, and she can cope with the more formal work:

> I wrote all this and then I opened the book again and this time . . . I didn't mind reading it

Now there are stylistic changes in her writing caused by her new attempt to marshall and reflect upon the information she possesses. As she progresses, the two halves of the writing, the personal and the impersonal, the informal and the formal, melt into each other, until it is impossible to separate them:

> I took a few notes from this book also, and found out that a red blood cell lasts 120 days and during this time travels about 700 miles. It gradually gets damaged as it's pushed along, and as it hasn't got a nucleus cannot repair itself and eventually bursts.

No-one told her to 'use your own words': she did when she had to, and wove them into the words of others. But the organisation is her own. If, as we have suggested, 'final writing' should be authentic communications, giving readers what they could only have got from that writer and enabling the writer to make new discoveries even in that final statement, then this piece on blood demonstrates the consequences of that kind of achievement.

Learning from books

I
I am watching three fourteen-year-old girls, who are looking at a workcard in a biology lesson. They are stuck on a question about the leg of a fly. 'Miss,' they say as their teacher arrives at their table, 'we don't know this.'

'Well,' says the teacher, 'get yourself a book from the shelf and look it up.' One of the girls goes for the book: when she returns she sits down and sighs. Then she opens the book at page one, and begins reading. After a minute her friend says impatiently, 'Oh, give it here.' She takes the book herself and turns to the contents page. She reads down it, then starts again. Then apparently giving up, she sits back and stares ahead of her.

I feel I ought to help. 'Why not try the index?' I suggest. The girl with the book looks at me, then starts leafing through the book. 'The index is usually at the back,' I say helpfully. She finds it, then runs her finger down the columns. She doesn't find 'leg of fly' under the 'L' column. 'Try "fly",' I say. 'It's not there,' she says.

'Can I have a look, please?' She passes me the book. As I begin to look at the index, I frown, and then look at the cover. The book is called *The Physiology of Plants*. 'You got the wrong book off the shelf,' I point out.

The whole process has taken ten minutes. They haven't found out what they had to – one could hardly say 'what they wanted to', because they were signally lacking in interest. When I tell the teacher afterwards she is shocked. 'But I assumed they'd know how to find things in books,' she says.

What she took for granted was that her pupils would be able to search for, retrieve, and use information from books; she assumed, as most of us do, that students would recognize by its title whether this book was appropriate or not; that they would know how to use an index; that they would be able to search rapidly for the right page or pages; and certainly would be able to identify the information they wanted when they found it.

But in this case, what the pupils did is as revealing as what they did not do; because this very ordinary event shows what happens if things are left to chance. Firstly, the pupil selected the wrong book. We do not know why she did, but clearly she had not scanned the shelves and checked the titles in the way we might expect. Nor had she used the topic of the question in any way to anticipate what the title of the book should be, or to help her to select the one that would be most helpful. That is not always as easy to do as it seems, either; although here it involves the obvious distinction between the physiology of plants and of animals or insects, at other times there are much subtler distinctions that can only be made when the searcher has previous knowledge and experience of the field of enquiry. For instance, in the example of the history class (on pp. 97ff) the teacher noticed that as the students worked on the essay about Mussolini, they passed over a book on Russian history from 1900–25: talking with them, he learned that because of their inexperience they had not seen the interrelationship between events and places that he had taken for granted, and thus had not bothered to look at that book. They had simply not known enough about Europe in the early twentieth century to recognize that the book on Russia might well have relevant material in it. Clearly students can't be expected to work only from titles when they are new to a topic.

Secondly, the girl who first used the book in the biology class began her search by apparently intending to read solidly through the text until she found the right chunk of information. No wonder she sighed! What she needed in her repertoire was the strategy that all experienced searchers for information possess – the quick skim through the text to look for the part that is wanted, using all available clues: chapter headings, key words in the text, illustrations and diagrams, paragraph beginnings and endings and so on. But before that, something that comes so automatically to the expert reader and researcher as to be almost below consciousness: the turning to the index, to see if the topic is mentioned at all, and if so, where.

A skim down the chapter headings might have told any of the girls that it was the wrong book. Her friend did that, but in that blank vacuum of helplessness that textbooks often generate, instead of recognizing that it *was* the wrong book she read it again, perhaps hoping that this time she would find the information she was looking for. When she was directed to the index, she uncovered an unexpected difficulty posed by the conventional conceptual index. Indexes classify: and their classifications subsume details under the main concept. Thus Hobsbawm and Rudé's book *Captain Swing* (1969) allows the reader to look up 'the grievances of agricultural labourers': it appears as 'labourers, agricultural . . . grievances of, 58'. But the girl looking up 'the leg of the fly' used the index as though it were a dictionary: she looked up 'leg' first, showing us what we might otherwise not have known – that coping with conceptual organization is not natural and inevitable, but depends upon a grasp of the hierarchical arrangement of the concepts being studied. If pupils are to use indexes and the other critical apparatus of books – bibliographies, footnotes, cross-references and so on – they need our active help, because they will not necessarily acquire the knowledge of how to use them by mere exposure to textbooks; especially if, like many second-rate school textbooks, the books lack that apparatus.

There is a final point about the biology workcard anecdote: the girls were bored by the whole business. Why should they want to find out anything about the leg of a fly, anyway? Well, the teacher had told them to, via the workcard, so, reluctantly, they did. But because they had no real purpose in searching for the information, except obeying that controlling dictate, it didn't matter to them if they found an answer or not: nor did it matter if they checked to see if this was the right book, the right page, or anything else.

II

The immediate and obvious lesson to be drawn from the incident of the biology workcard is that the techniques of using books to find information are not unconsciously absorbed but need to be deliberately provided for. Sometimes children *may* learn them, accidentally, so to speak; but most will need to be helped to acquire them. Once we are aware of that, we can easily find opportunities for doing something about it.

But there is a deeper lesson, which connects reading for learning with all the other uses of language for learning in this book: that is, that the student needs to feel a sense of inner purpose in reading as in writing and talking, and that when that sense of purpose is present, what students can achieve in their reading may be as striking, though not as visible, as the other achievements described in this book. When it is not present, when, that is, the drive is entirely from the teacher's purpose instead of from the students', then it is not enough for the students to have been 'taught the skills'. Although it is true that there is one aspect to the process which is almost mechanical and can be instilled by instruction in techniques, that technique is only fully deployed in the context of a real search, with a real intention to find something out; and real searches are characteristic of a whole distinctive climate of learning and relationships in which students are in the habit of seeking answers to questions, assisted by teachers who help them to find the answers in books. Sometimes, indeed, if their purpose is powerful enough, the students will instruct themselves: Billy Casper's experience (Hines 1969) of searching laboriously for information he badly wanted, is not unique. Often, reports of experiences like Billy Casper's are regarded with suspicion as false or idealized; but the surprise that is commonly expressed about 'poor readers' who do read material that is important to them, suggests that there are factors at work which deserve to be taken seriously. A label like 'poor reader' tends to imply a permanent condition. But when we investigate, we find how crucial to their performance is the self-regard of the readers, and how that self-regard is affected by what happens at school and at home. The eleven-year-old girl who writes: 'I prefer being at home to being at school because at home I am not a non-reader' tells us something important about the way she will react in school, as a person who feels diminished and demeaned by the label applied to her. The same feeling comes from ten-year-old Mandy, who writes:

I don't like reading because of the questions, but I read because I think it mite make me go on to library one day. . . . Once when I was in Mrs M's class I read a book all the way through and she put me all the way back to the front, and I at to read it again I didn't like that very much

Mandy is a 'poor reader'; and not surprisingly, if what she normally reads are cards and comprehension passages with 'questions'. But that is not, in fact, all that she reads:

I like reading fairy storys and sometimes love storys. I like reading whats on television

Donny, in the same class, is also a 'poor reader'; but in his case, only in school:

> I read the tellygraph [at home] and when I get stuck I ask my brother. I like reading I read more at home than I do at school...

Dennis Lawrence (1973) has pointed out that problems with reading are sometimes caused by matters which have nothing to do with reading itself, and suggests that they may be resolved by counselling rather than direct teaching of reading. But they may also be functions of the difficulty and nature of what is provided for the children to read; or of the purposes for which students are expected to read in school. And they may equally be caused by the environment in which the reading takes place, and the environment includes the way in which the student is regarded by the teacher.

When the environment is favourable and material is provided that meets the students' current preoccupations, then apparent difficulties can disappear. Some anecdotes about four children, all regarded as 'poor readers', demonstrate this point:

> A nine-year-old 'non-reader' wanted to find out what to feed the caterpillar he had found. He had to find the right book, identify the caterpillar, and having found out what plant it fed on, locate where that plant grew in the local environment.

> A thirteen-year-old boy whose class was shown Dali's 'Christ of St John on the Cross' became fascinated by the picture. On a visit to an art gallery, his teacher bought him a small book on Dali, on whom he became an expert.

> A fourteen-year-old 'remedial' girl was put in charge of the guinea-pigs in the biology laboratory, and given a book about them to help her feed and care for them. Eventually, she wrote her own manual which was kept in the laboratory for future keepers.

> A seven-year-old boy, able to read, but very reluctant to, became intrigued by sea-shells while on holiday, and collected large numbers of them. Provided with *The Hamlyn*

Guide to the Seashore and Shallow Seas (Campbell 1976)
he became expert at identifying and knowing about the shells
he found.

In all these cases, the students were considered to be poor
readers, but had purposes which gave them reasons to search
for the information, because it answered the questions they were
asking themselves. But they also had climates which supported
them, and which, by recognizing their individual directions,
provided them with the right material when it was most relevant.

III

Readers can want to unlock the contents of a book if they have a
question they urgently want answered, or a consuming desire to
know more about a topic. What is more, with needs like those,
readers can find they can cope with material which is supposed
to be out of their reach. Purpose is what makes that possible;
but it is also purpose, in a broad sense, that makes *any* reading
possible, not just coping with the organized complexity of a
book's arrangement to retrieve information. In most reading,
though, the 'purpose' is more diffuse, and less identifiable, and
could better be expressed as 'expectation'. The reader who gets
meaning from a text is the one who expects to find meaning in
it: that expectation is both a prediction and an intention.
Successful readers (whatever their ability as measured by stan-
dardized tests) are those who begin by knowing that there will
be meaning on the page, that however unwelcoming the surface
there is a voice residing in the text that tells us something we
want to hear; and that what the book is doing is something that
is basically familiar, like what we do when we listen to people
telling us things, or perhaps when we think about something.

Starting from that basic trust in the text, we let it take over
and find ourselves listening to, even thinking, someone else's
words. With 'easy' texts, our eyes run along the printed words,
and the thoughts and ideas – the meanings – happen in our head
without much difficulty. We may have to read more demanding
texts more than once: the meaning emerges gradually, or piece-
meal in fits and starts. We ascribe meaning to the sentences and
the elements within the sentences as far as we can, calling on our
existing fund of knowledge and experience to help us make sense
of this new material. This enables us to form a provisional sense
of the meaning of the whole thing; and that total meaning in

turn modifies the meanings we ascribe to the bits. We play against each other the sense we make of the parts and of the whole, so that they reciprocally modify each other, and thus we move towards an understanding of the whole text. We match that understanding with what we already know, so that the two meanings modify and are modified by each other. But whether the process is fluent or laborious, it is our expectation that there is a meaning there that enables us to carry it through.

Reading information books is *not*, therefore, simply a matter of accumulating meaning by the successive reception of bits as the words are decoded, one by one. One obvious proof of this is that a major part of the meaning of a text resides in the relationship of one sentence to another, yet there is often little in the text to signal those relationships (Halliday and Hasan 1976). Those who have an inadequate sense of what reading is and approach it as cumulative decoding instead of as a search for the author's sense, do not get very far.

What we have said about reading, placing *purpose* at its centre, indicates how the same considerations apply to it as to learning in general. What is more, the successful reader who is grappling with a demanding text goes through the general learning processes we have proposed. Learners make their own associations with 'the elements', the things the information is about, and do it by bringing together what they know already and the new material being met for the first time; interests and concerns are brought into play; and the readers speculate, silently or aloud or in writing, about the implications of what is being read. For although in a way the author's thoughts are being thought in our minds when we read, another part of us remains under our own control to answer back, criticize and evaluate.

IV

We have said before that the processes which we observe occurring in our own thoughts can sometimes be profitably induced to take place interpersonally, between people, in talking or writing. Similarly, we can help students to control their own reading by interpersonal work on texts, or by other devices which make the processes explicit. Students working through a text in pairs or groups, talking as they go, may understand it more successfully than solitary readers because they are sharing their pooled experiences. The geography example on p. 104 shows that happening; and the two examples of group discussion of poems, which lend themselves particularly to this treatment, show extended discussion taking place to support and assist with reading. Informative texts can be handled in the same way. A group of fifth-year girls were preparing an essay on 'Why did the Axis powers lose the war?'. They had used their notes and textbooks to collect information, and now take stock:

1	*Anne*	So let's see what we've got now then we've got Hitler with all his troops everywhere in Europe and erm towards the end of the War we've got America joining
2	*Jeanette*	Yeah
3	*Anne*	Hitler's troops are running out mmm so really the Allies are becoming stronger and winning the war (yeah) if you get what I mean (laughs) right – erm –
4	*Alison*	A lot of it's because of Italy really wasn't it?
5	*Anne*	A lot of it yeah that's that's explaining why Hitler had to go on helping Mussolini over lands which didn't really matter
6	*Alison*	Yeah really I don't think he really expected that he'd have to run after Italy so much really (no) when you think about it
7	*Jeanette*	Oh hold it

Jeanette, vaguely remembering something, begins to leaf back through her books. Anne and Alison continue their discussion until in a moment or two she finds what she was looking for in one of the books in front of them:

14	*Jeanette*	I think it was a change of government wasn't it in Britain that affected it really

They are fairly advanced learners making little distinction between what they know already and what they are gathering from the books: they fit it together, and it all serves to focus in on the problem they are trying to solve. Because it was presented as a problem, and because they have learnt from their teacher to take questions like this seriously, they successfully engage with complex reading, and make it serve their purpose. But they are able to do it because their teacher has also encouraged them to do collaboratively, in talk, the searching for evidence and the evaluation of it as potential evidence: to have done that on their own, at their stage, may well have been too difficult.

There are other ways of examining their own processes of reading which are helpful to learners. A group of A-level biology students were reading a section of a textbook which dealt with a new topic (see p. 133). Their teacher asked them to read it with a piece of paper alongside, and to jot down any questions or thoughts they had. Two things resulted: they were able to verbalize what usually remains latent, the dialogue between book and reader; but also, the strategy generated more connections, speculations and hypotheses than would normally have occurred. Because they were consciously interrogating the text instead of accepting it passively, they questioned more; and their questions and statements show the processes they were going through: trying to understand at a basic level:

> But how do they get into the blood? What do they look like? (Sue)
>
> What are endocrine glands? (Jayne)

trying to understand functions:

> Does the response depend on the amount of hormone released? How are they transported? (Margot)
>
> How does the thyroid synthesize thyroxin? (Jayne)

But they also see subtle implications, not derived directly from the text, but created by the interaction of their previous knowledge with these new ideas:

> Can it be proved that they have the same evolutionary origin? (Jayne)
>
> If 'target organs' are equivalent to effectors in nerves, is there a 'synapse' controlling their production or effectiveness? (Margot)

And in at least one case, one of the students identified an idea that startled her, and the rest of the group when they discussed it later:

> Chemical transmission? – susceptible to drugs?! (Margot)

Hormonal communication

Hormones are organic compounds produced in one part of the body, from which they are transported to other parts where they produce a response. A minute quantity may exert a profound effect on the organism's development, structure or behaviour. Here we shall only be concerned with the general principles involved.

Hormones are secreted by **endocrine organs** directly into the bloodstream. The word endocrine means 'internal secretion' and the endocrine organs are therefore **glands of internal secretion**. Since they shed their secretion into the bloodstream, they have no ducts and are hence known as **ductless glands**. Once in the bloodstream, the hormones are carried round the body, bringing about responses in various places. Structures that respond to them are called **target organs**.

Though they may be widely separated from one another spatially, endocrine organs do not exist in functional isolation. They influence one another and, through their interactions, are integrated into a highly coordinated system, the **endocrine system**. . .

Despite these obvious differences, there is one fundamental similarity between the two systems: both involve **chemical transmission**. We saw earlier that in the nervous system transmission of the message across the neuromuscular junctions is achieved by a chemical substance. The latter is equivalent to a hormone in the endocrine system. The principal difference between them is that the neuromuscular transmitter has to travel a mere fraction of . . .

Biology: A Functional Approach M. B. V. Roberts, Nelson 1976

Their discussion led them to consider the widespread use of drugs by doctors, and to try to work out the possible consequences.

This is an example of one way in which writing can help with reading: private unstructured jottings of associations and provisional meanings, or diagrams of arguments, a symbolic representation of what is on the page rather than a verbal one, are ways in which writing can help in understanding, and also give students an increasing confidence in themselves as learners, as they find that their associations and questions are taken seriously by the teacher and their peers.

There are other techniques which can be used (Lunzer and Gardner 1979, Walker 1976); and strategies like controlling the pace and sequencing the process in order to establish techniques may be important ways of helping the learner. 'Skim through this for one minute; jot down one line to say what it's about; read it again for 3–4 minutes: were you right? Now write down three or four subheadings for the passage', and so on.

There are, it is clear, several ways in which we can provide our students with the kind of support they need to cope with the texts we offer them. And by making explicit to pupils exactly what elements of reading are called into play by the various strategies we can make it easier for them to move towards independence, and be able to cope alone. But we need also to pay attention to the texts themselves, because they too can pose particular problems.

V

We know that, given the urgent purpose we have discussed above, students can read what appears to be too difficult; but we cannot expect such intense focussing in every run-of-the-mill encounter with written texts. So we need to see that the texts we provide are the kind of material our students stand a chance of reading. A high proportion of what is put before students is quite simply inaccessible to them; a new awareness of this has been accompanied by considerable interest, both in Britain and the United States, in measures of 'readability' (Gilliland 1972) and as Colin Harrison points out (Lunzer and Gardner 1979) there are many different formulae for assessing how 'readable' texts are. Most of the formulae depend on certain objective measures, mainly sentence length and the incidence of long words (that is, words of three or more syllables). But there are problems in using readability formulae for anything but alerting one to possible difficulties in the most general way. It does not seem possible at all to use them to assess literature: *A Farewell to Arms*, for instance, according to the formulae, has a 'readability age' of around nine years; but what would even the most sophisticated nine-year-old reader make of the final words of the novel, where Lieutenant Henry's wife has just died in childbirth?

> I went to the door of the room.
> 'You can't come in now,' one of the nurses said.
> 'Yes, I can,' I said.
> 'You can't come in yet.'
> 'You get out,' I said. 'The other one too.'
> But after I had got them out and shut the door and turned off the light it wasn't any good. It was like saying goodbye to a statue. After a while I went out and left the hospital and walked back to the hotel in the rain.

The short sentences and simple words are intended to create a particular emotional atmosphere and response in the reader, not to give it a low 'readability age'. The readability index of a text does not necessarily indicate that children of that age will be able to read it. In this case, the surface meaning of the words may be accessible to the young reader, but the full meaning of the text is beyond them because of the nature of that meaning.

What about the application of readability formulae to non-narrative books? Well, even here the problem is not as simple as the formulae can make it appear. Here are three sentences which pose problems of understanding for most of us, but for different reasons:

1   A sealed-bearing bottom bracket unit with a titanium axle is available . . . to fit Campagnola, Dura-Ace and SR Royal crank arms.

    Richard's Bicycle Book, R. Ballantyne, Pan 1975

2   In a full grammar of English there would be a very large number of subclasses of verbs, categorized in terms of the syntactic environment in which they occur.

    J. P. B. Allen and H. G. Widdowson 'Grammar and

language teaching' in *Papers in Applied Linguistics* J. P. B. Allen and S. Pit Corder (eds), OUP 1975

3   The man who involves himself and who realizes that he is not only the person he chooses to be, but also a law-maker who is, at the same time, choosing all mankind as well as himself, cannot help escape the feeling of his total and deep responsibility.

Jean Paul Sartre 'Existentialism' in *Existentialism and Human Emotions*

The first of these passages poses problems that would be solved simply, by knowing the things to which the words refer – bottom-bracket, titanium axle, a crank arm, SR Royal. Once one knew these things, the passage would be intelligible. The second is more complex: one might look up, if one needed to, 'syntactic' and 'verbs', but even then the meaning of the whole is greater than the sum of its parts: the full implications only emerge to those who already possess background knowledge which is relevant. The third example, though, is puzzling. Each word is simple and familiar; but what can the whole thing mean? And what does 'choosing all mankind as well as himself', in particular, mean?

The examples offer three different aspects of difficulty in texts. The first is the simplest: if we do not know the things that the words refer to, we will find the words puzzling. Or we may know the things, but not have known that those were their names. The second is difficult because the unfamiliar words relate not to simple referents, to things, but to systems of concepts and related ideas. This is the kind of problem that school textbooks may pose, and it is the most common 'readability' problem in education, because students spend much of their time meeting new ideas and new words which represent the visible one-tenth of a whole system of meaning. But the third example represents the most formidable problem, because it may not be obvious to the person who does understand it that there is anything difficult about it. There are no specialized words, no technical concepts: but when highly complex ideas are expressed in simple, familiar language then there is normally a problem of understanding, not because of difficult words or complex syntax, but because of difficult *ideas*. Meaning becomes slippery and elusive and the struggle to understand becomes itself an act of learning.

VI

Once learners know that they can expect, as a matter of course, to get meaning from written language, then reading becomes accessible to them in a way that has some correspondences with the way spoken language is accessible. The reader needs to feel that there will be a recognizable voice that speaks from the words on the page, and is interested in conveying something directly to the reader. Clearly, then, the process of reading is a process of interaction between a text that has something to say and a reader who wants to hear it. This means that there are qualities that ought to inhere in the text. Many informational books have no discernible voice in them, nor have the authors seen it as part of a writer's role to address themselves to the difficulties that students face in getting at the information, beyond trying to write simply and clearly, and furnishing explanations at the points where they seem to be needed: and only the best of them do that. One important role of teachers lies in their selection of material in the first place. Books get into schools not because the children express interest in them, but because they are ordered by the staff, and the criteria used to decide on which book to purchase are not always as clearcut as they might be. The essential characteristics of an information book should be that it should genuinely set out to convey information, rather than to 'occupy' classes; that ideally it should be information that is felt directly by the writer, rather than second-order stuff culled from other people's books; that as a matter of course it should include index, bibliography, and the normal apparatus of 'real' books; and that the readers should recognize the language of the book as being essentially the same sort of thing as the spoken language. This last point, in particular, needs further comment.

We have argued that in children's own writing there should be a continuity between the written language which is close to their own speech and the organized public language they must learn to operate. We have suggested that their language should be seen as developing so that as they get older it gradually comes to exhibit, in appropriate situations, features of mature transactional language. In the written language of others which they encounter, there should be the same continuity. It should not be the case, as it so often is, that the only written language the students encounter in (for example) science or history, is of the type most remote from speech, most remote from the language they produce themselves. There needs to be language that they can identify with, and in which they can detect communicative and expressive purposes like their own. As writers themselves, they will be able to learn most from writing which is within reach of their own, or is at least an expression of recognizably similar intentions. For instance, here is the beginning of a book on archaeology. A dry subject, perhaps, often written about in an arid way. But this opening, with its personal voice, immediately establishes that the writer (Magnusson 1972) is moved by feelings which we can share, so that even if we know nothing about its topic, we want to read on. The first chapter is called 'What is archaeology?'.

> I call it my talisman, my lucky token, and it always sits on the desk in front of me. It is my most treasured possession; and yet it is worth nothing at all – just an ordinary stone, about the size and shape of a pear. . . . Both ends of the stone, the blunt end and the sharper end, showed signs of having been chipped; and on the surface of the stone were some irregular dark patches, like grease-marks. When I hold the stone in my hand, these grease-marks fit exactly the flesh-pads of my palm and fingers, because these dark marks, I was assured, had been made by sweat; they were the grimy sweat-marks of people who had used the stone as a primitive hammer all those long centuries ago.

That tone of voice should be among the voices that students hear as they explore their subjects, and it is not as rare as it might seem. Once we start looking outside the narrow and often restricting confines of textbooks, we find writing of high quality that compels us to pay attention to the writer. Not only that, it leads us into a subject in ways that school textbooks never can. Here is the beginning of an essay 'On Warts': it is interesting, accessible, and lively:

> Warts are wonderful structures. They can appear overnight on any part of the skin, like mushrooms on a damp lawn,

full grown and splendid in the complexity of their architecture. Viewed in stained sections under a microscope, they are the most specialised of cellular arrangements, constructed as though for a purpose. They sit there like turreted mounds of dense, impenetrable horn, impregnable, designed for defense against the world outside.

In a certain sense, warts are both useful and essential, but not for us. As it turns out, the exuberant cells of a wart are the elaborate apparatus of a virus.

You might have thought from the looks of it that the cells infected by the wart virus were using this response as a ponderous way of defending themselves against the virus, maybe even a way of becoming more distasteful, but it is not so. The wart is what the virus truly wants; it can flourish only in cells undergoing precisely this kind of overgrowth. It is not a defense at all; it is an overwhelming welcome, an enthusiastic accommodation meeting the needs of more and more virus.

The strangest thing about warts is that they tend to go away. Fully grown, nothing in the body has so much the look of toughness and permanence as a wart, and yet, inexplicably and often very abruptly, they come to the end of their lives and vanish without a trace. (Thomas 1980)

If as writers students need models they can identify with, then as learners they need rich experience in the elements of a topic; they need the same knowledge presented to them in various ways so that by seeing it in different contexts, they see its different implications. They need to see the knowledge as perceived through different eyes, handled both personally and impersonally. So the classroom needs to contain a variety of reading materials selected on the principle that anything well written which is related to the topic in hand is worth having around. The sources will need to extend well beyond what can be obtained from educational catalogues: the material is to be found in journals, diaries, biographies and autobiographical extracts, letters, newspapers, novels, poems, magazine interviews, writing by other students, transcripts of student discussions, comics, a range of textbooks, and writing by the teacher. And just as in their general approach to learning students need to range widely around the territory in which the topic is located, so in relation to reading material, they need to be able to browse and make their own selections as well as reading for immediate and defined purposes. The best basis for teaching and learning is a reading experience which constantly alternates between detailed and wide-ranging, between intensive and extensive, between meeting study needs and following up broad interests. Thus the teacher can lead students into the vast library of resources in which it is hoped they will come to feel at home.

A climate for learning

If you go into a school or into someone else's classroom, what you notice isn't the educational theory of the teacher, or the rigour of the curriculum. You see people, doing things and behaving in particular ways. You notice if they're interested or not in what they are doing, because if they're not there is likely to be noise and particular kinds of behaviour. You also notice how the teacher and the learners behave towards each other, how they talk to each other and look at each other. How cheerful and lived-in, looked-after and interesting the room is, how the tables and chairs or desks are set out, what's on the walls – all these things you notice. In other words, what you're conscious of is not intellectual abstractions like timetabling, syllabuses, or organizational structures but the climate of the school as a place to live in. And a school is lived in: it isn't just a setting for a specialized process. Teachers and students live in it together for at least 1100 hours a year.

A climate that is good to live in can also be a climate in which learning flourishes: certainly, a learning climate needs first to be a living climate – because living and learning are not distinct activities. It is the product of the countless specific actions of teachers and students, and not something achieved by legislation. In particular, it is the product of the language that occurs in the normal day-to-day business of teaching, learning and social living together. There is no separation between an individual and that individual's language: not only are 'the limits of my language the limits of my world', but 'what you say is what you are'. There are deeply rooted connections between personality, learning and language, and what touches one touches all: invaders seeking to eradicate troublesome individuality in subject peoples, first forbid the local, indigenous language, Welsh or Breton, and impose their own. In the same way, particular forms of language enable authority to exert control, people to express self-respect and regard for each other, ideas to be expressed, and the transactions of everyday life to be conducted.

In the course of this book, you have seen examples of ordinary boys and girls in several parts of the country demonstrating that they can learn, can take knowledge seriously, and can derive from it the satisfactions that are sometimes felt to be confined to the 'most able'. The climates they lived and worked in put those achievements within their grasp. Knowledge was taken seriously: teachers passed it on not as a matter of school routine but because they themselves, in a way that was apparent to the students, found it of value. They saw to it that the knowledge that was introduced was the best and most up-to-date available, derived from their own reading as well as from the textbook. The teachers themselves, by choosing still to be learners, were evidence for the students that the knowledge was worth the effort to acquire. They were serious, too, in their determination that *all* their students should be able to experience the knowledge for themselves. Ethically speaking, if a person's freedom is removed by enforced attendance at school, then this can be justified only if the most clearcut benefits result. Teachers need to demonstrate by the way they think and feel that for them knowledge bestows a power they would not be without; and that their intention is to make the same knowledge, and therefore power, available to their students.

But the teachers' commitment to the knowledge is not on its own sufficient: as we've seen, good teaching in the conventional sense does not guarantee good learning. What is noteworthy about the classrooms described here is that there is also a free traffic in information, ideas, and opinions. All the participants in this climate have access to all the channels of communication: teachers and learners exchange and share ideas, all are receptive and hospitable to what others have to say. Speculation and imagination thrive because the dialogue between learner and teacher encourages it: language exists in a variety of forms because the complexity of the ideas being handled inevitably generates variation in what is expressed. Real books and periodicals as well as textbooks, talk in large and small groups, stories and poems as well as essays and notes, the racy vernacular and the well-wrought composition, and a constant recognition of the real world inside and outside the school: these form the backbone of the language-life of the school.

Above all, relationships are characterized by mutuality; 'All real living is meeting' said Buber (1937): and the language transactions that characterize the climate of learning are exchanges of authentic messages from individuals speaking in their own right. Students are self-regarding autonomous agents with their own valid concerns and styles and are free to initiate as well as to follow. Teachers recognize that however they teach, the students have to make their own knowledge – there is no other way. So they encourage this: and as the students work on their own constructions of knowledge, they help them. They do this, not in any authoritarian way, insisting that the students accept the teacher's view, but as people with experiences and alternative viewpoints to be set alongside the students' own ideas. This is no abdication: it involves an insistence that the teachers should be recognized by the students, as the students are by them. The essential is that, in terms of the right to judge for themselves and to express what they see – if not in expertise and understanding – teachers and students stand side by side as equals facing the same reality; and so students trust teachers not only with the final outcomes of their learning but with their doubts, perplexities, ignorance and speculations.

That would all seem pious, wishful thinking if it were not that, as you have seen, it is perfectly possible. Moreover, once tasted, it becomes essential. Once students and teachers have experienced that climate of triangular engagement between self, others and the outside world of experience and ideas, then they are unlikely to be satisfied with anything less: there is a spiralling commitment, deriving not only from external rewards and prospects of qualifications, but from the satisfactions of perceiving patterns where there was merely the flux of sensation and experience.

'Implementing a language policy' is an unfortunate phrase for what schools need to do to create this kind of climate. It suggests that clearcut decisions can be made which can be immediately put into effect by simple agreement. It is not like that at all. The changes needed are not merely technical ones. Schools which agree on common procedures for marking spelling mistakes, introducing technical terms, and vetting worksheets for 'readability' are making useful first steps; but the heart of the matter lies elsewhere. What ultimately makes the difference between students half-engaged and students committed to learning is the climate of the classroom and beyond that of the school.

Bibliography

ABERCROMBIE, M. J. L. (1969) *The Anatomy of Judgment* Penguin

BARNES, D., BRITTON, J. and ROSEN, H. (1971) *Language, the Learner and the School* Penguin

BELLACK, A. A., KLIEBARD, H. M., HYMAN, R. T. and SMITH, F. L. (1966) *The Language of the Classroom* New York: Teachers College Press

BETTELHEIM, B. (1977) *The Uses of Enchantment* Thames and Hudson

BLACKIE, P. (1971) Asking questions *English in Education* 5, 3

BRITTON, J. *et al.* (1975) *The Development of Writing Abilities 11–18* Macmillan Education for the Schools Council

BUBER, M. (1937) *I and Thou* (trans. R. Smith) Clark

BURGESS, C. *et al.* (1973) *Understanding Children Writing* Penguin

CASSIRER, E. (1946) *Language and Myth* Dover

DES (1975) *A Language for Life* (The Bullock Report) HMSO

DOUGHTY, P., PEARCE, J. and THORNTON, G. (1972) *Exploring Language* Edward Arnold

DUNSBEE, T. and FORD, T. (1980) *Mark My Words* Ward Lock Educational

EINSTEIN, A. (1960) *Relativity* Methuen

FRIEDLANDER, K. (1947) Children's books and their function in latency and prepuberty/puberty *American Imago* 3, 2

GILLILAND, J. (1972) *Readability* Hodder

HALLIDAY, M. and HASAN, R. (1976) *Cohesion in Texts* Longman

HARDING, D. W. (1963) *Experience into Words* Chatto and Windus

HARGREAVES, D. (1967) *Social Relations in the Secondary School* Routledge & Kegan Paul

HARGREAVES, D. *et al.* (1975) *Deviance in Classrooms* Routledge & Kegan Paul

HINES, B. (1969) *A Kestrel for a Knave* Penguin

HOBSBAWM, E. J. and RUDÉ, G. (1973) *Captain Swing* Penguin

HOWE, M. J. A. (1977) *Adult Learning* Wiley

JACKSON, B. and MARSDEN, D. (1966) *Education and the Working Class* Penguin

KELLY, G. (1963) *A Theory of Personality* New York: Norton

LAWRENCE, D. (1973) *Improving Reading through Counselling* Ward Lock Educational

LUNZER, E. and GARDNER, K. (1979) *The Effective Use of Reading* Heinemann Educational for the Schools Council

MAGNUSSON, M. (1972) *Introducing Archaeology* Bodley Head

MARTIN, N. *et al.* (1976) *Writing and Learning Across the Curriculum* Ward Lock Educational

MARTIN, N. *et al.* (1977) *Language Policies in Schools* Ward Lock Educational

McLEOD, A. (1976) 'This is what came out' in M. Torbe and R. Protherough *Classroom Encounters* (eds) Ward Lock Educational

MEDWAY, P. (1980) *Finding a Language : autonomy and learning in School* Writers and Readers Publishing Cooperative in association with Chameleon

MOFFETT, J. (1968) *Teaching the Universe of Discourse* Boston: Houghton Mifflin

PIAGET, J. (1959) *Language and Thought of the Child* Routledge & Kegan Paul

POLANYI, M. (1973) *Personal Knowledge* Routledge & Kegan Paul

ROSEN, H. (1973) Written language and the sense of audience *Educational Research* 15, 3

SAPIR, E. (1961) *Culture, Language and Personality* Berkley, California: University of California Press

SINCLAIR, J. M. and COULTHARD, R. M. (1975) *Towards an Analysis of Discourse* Oxford University Press

SMITH, F. (1971) *Understanding Reading* Holt, Rinehart and Winston

THOMAS, L. (1980) 'On Warts' in *The Medusa and the Snail* New York: Bantam Books

THOMPSON, E. P. (1971) *The Making of the English Working Class* Penguin

TORBE, M. (1976) *Language across the Curriculum : Guidelines for Schools* Ward Lock Educational for NATE

VYGOTSKY, L. S. (1962) *Thought and Language* Boston: MIT Press

WALKER, C (1976) *Reading Extension and Development* Ward Lock Educational

YOUNG, M. F. D. (1974) *Knowledge and Control* Collier-Macmillan

Index

Index by Ann Edwards